Matthew 5–7

How to Be Happy

A Guided Discovery for Groups and Individuals

Kevin Perrotta

LoyolaPress.
A Jesuit Ministry
Chicago

LOYOLAPRESS.
A JESUIT MINISTRY

3441 N. Ashland Avenue
Chicago, Illinois 60657
(800) 621-1008
www.loyolapress.com

Nihil Obstat
Reverend John Lodge, S.T.D.
Censor Deputatus
June 3, 2002

Imprimatur
Most Reverend Raymond E. Goedert, M.A., S.T.L., J.C.L.
Vicar General
Archdiocese of Chicago
June 6, 2002

The *Nihil Obstat* and *Imprimatur* are official declarations that a book is free of doctrinal and moral error. No implication is contained therein that those who have granted the *Nihil Obstat* and *Imprimatur* agree with the content, opinions, or statements expressed. Nor do they assume any legal responsibility associated with publication.

The excerpt from the *Catechism of the Catholic Church* (p. 39) is taken from the second edition (Washington, D.C.: United States Catholic Conference, 1997), 499–501.

The comments by Bud Welch (p. 51) are used with his permission.

The Latin text of St. Augustine's comments on the Our Father (p. 64–65) can be found in Almut Mutzenbecher, ed., *Sancti Aurelii Augustini: De Sermone Domini in Monte Libros Duos,* Corpus Christianorum Series Latina, vol. 35 (Turnhout, Belgium: Typographi Brepols, 1962). An English version may be found in St. Augustine, *The Lord's Sermon on the Mount,* Ancient Christian Writers, no. 5, trans. John J. Jepson, S.S. (New York: Newman Press, 1948). The translation in this book is by Kevin Perrotta.

The excerpt from St. Athanasius's biography of St. Anthony of Egypt (p. 75) is adapted from the translation of the works of Athanasius on the Christian Classics Ethereal Library Web site (www.ccel.org).

The narrative by Ann Shields (p. 87) first appeared in *Pastoral Renewal* (November 1986). Used with author's permission.

Interior design by Kay Hartmann/Communique Design
Illustration by Charise Mericle Harper

ISBN-13: 978-0-8294-1814-9; ISBN-10: 0-8294-1814-8

Printed in the United States of America
14 Bang 10

Contents

How to Use This Guide

You might compare the Bible to a national park. The park is so large that you could spend months, even years, getting to know it. But a brief visit, if carefully planned, can be enjoyable and worthwhile. In a few hours you can drive through the park and pull over at a handful of sites. At each stop you can get out of the car, take a short trail through the woods, listen to the wind blowing through the trees, get a feel for the place.

In this booklet we'll travel through a small portion of the Bible—chapters 5 through 7 of Matthew's Gospel, Jesus' Sermon on the Mount. Because the sermon is short, we will be able to take a leisurely walk through it, thinking carefully about what we are reading and what it means for our lives today. Although the sermon is short, it gives us a great deal to reflect on.

This guide provides everything you need to explore the Sermon on the Mount in six discussions—or to do a six-part exploration on your own. The introduction on page 6 will prepare you to get the most out of your reading. The weekly sections provide explanations that highlight what Jesus' words mean for us today. Equally important, each section supplies questions that will launch your group into fruitful discussion, helping you to both investigate Jesus' teaching for yourself and learn from one another. If you're using the booklet by yourself, the questions will spur your personal reflection.

Each discussion is meant to be a *guided discovery.*

Guided. None of us is equipped to read the Bible without help. We read the Bible *for* ourselves but not *by* ourselves. Scripture was written to be understood and applied in the community of faith. So each week "A Guide to the Reading," drawing on the work of both modern biblical scholars and Christian writers of the past, supplies background and explanations. The guide will help you grasp Jesus' message. Think of it as a friendly park ranger who points out noteworthy details and explains what you're looking at so you can appreciate things for yourself.

Discovery. The purpose is for *you* to interact with Jesus' teaching. "Questions for Careful Reading" is a tool to help you dig into the text and examine it carefully. "Questions for Application" will help you consider what these words mean for your life here and now. Each week concludes with an "Approach to Prayer" section that helps you respond to God's word. Supplementary "Living Tradition" and "Saints in the Making" sections offer the thoughts and experiences of Christians past and present. By showing what this sermon has meant to others, these sections will help you consider what it means for you.

How long are the discussion sessions? We've assumed you will have about an hour and a half when you get together. If you have less time, you'll find that most of the elements can be shortened somewhat.

Is homework necessary? You will get the most out of your discussions if you read the weekly material and prepare your answers to the questions in advance of each meeting. If participants are not able to prepare, have someone read the "Guide to the Reading" sections aloud to the group at the points where they appear. (Notice, however, that the "Guide to the Reading" in Week 1 is longer than usual—probably too long for reading aloud at the discussion session.) "Between Discussions" pages offer supplementary material to be read outside group sessions.

What about leadership? If you happen to have a world-class biblical scholar in your group, by all means ask him or her to lead the discussions. But in the absence of any professional Scripture scholars, or even accomplished amateur biblical scholars, you can still have a first-class Bible discussion. Choose two or three people to take turns as facilitators and have everyone read "Suggestions for Bible Discussion Groups" (page 92) before beginning.

Does everyone need a guide? a Bible? Everyone in the group will need their own copy of this booklet. It contains the entire text of the Sermon on the Mount, so a Bible is not absolutely necessary—but each participant will find it useful to have one (some of the questions refer to other parts of the Bible). You should have at least one Bible on hand for your discussions. (See page 96 for recommendations.)

How do we get started? Before you begin, take a look at the suggestions for Bible discussion groups (page 92) or individuals (page 95).

Life with a Purpose

In a typically American juxtaposition, St. Agnes Church, which looks like it was designed to stand in an alpine valley, towers over a neighborhood of homes belonging, for the most part, to African Americans, Native Americans, and Hmong people from Laos. German-speaking immigrants built the St. Paul, Minnesota, church in the 1800s. Its graceful clock tower and gleaming baroque interior, with subdued golden accents and elegant stained-glass windows, perfectly reflected the builders' central European piety and taste. But their descendants moved away long ago. The church and its school now serve a mixed twenty-first-century population.

Two of my daughters were among the mix of young people who made their way through St. Agnes high school in recent years. On Sunday afternoons two years apart, first Anna, then Virginia donned a graduation gown and joined the procession down the church's main aisle, beneath a lofty ceiling painting of the teen martyr Agnes being welcomed by angels into heaven. On both occasions, the church's pastor, Monsignor Richard Schuler, delivered pretty much the same short message. The gist of it was simply "God created you to be happy." What an appropriate reassurance for young adults launching out into a changing world!

Monsignor, I'm sure, would readily acknowledge that he took his theme from a Jewish preacher who addressed audiences long before Africans, Germans, or Laotians came to America. Speaking to gatherings of people in first-century Palestine, Jesus of Nazareth not only asserted that God had created them to be happy; he announced that God was acting in a fresh way to secure their happiness. And he instructed them in the way of living by which they could find the happiness that God intended for them. What a vital message for them—and for you and me today.

Jesus himself did not write down his thoughts. But after his death, his followers gathered their recollections into orderly accounts of his life and teaching. In one of these accounts, the Gospel of Matthew, the sermon that we will be reading over the next six weeks is featured as Jesus' inaugural speech. Because of the location where Jesus delivered his sermon, it is called the Sermon on the Mount.

Because the Sermon on the Mount is not an independent work but part of Matthew's Gospel, we should view it within the whole story that Matthew tells. Matthew opens with a narrative of Jesus' birth and infancy, then fast-forwards some thirty years to a scene at the Jordan River, where Jesus is baptized by a prophet known as John the Baptist (chapters 1–3; unless otherwise noted, biblical citations in this book refer to Matthew's Gospel). Immediately afterward, Jesus spends some weeks in the dry hills east of Jerusalem, praying, fasting, and being tested by the devil (4:1–11). Matthew's accounts of Jesus' birth, baptism, and temptation converge like spotlights on the subject of his identity: together the events show Jesus to be God's unique and obedient Son (1:20; 3:17; 4:3, 6). Thus Jesus deserves to be believed when he begins to announce that a new phase in God's saving activity is underway (4:17).

Jesus gathers disciples (4:18–22) and soon attracts crowds by his remarkable healing powers (4:23–25). Then, at an outdoor venue somewhere in Galilee—the northern region of present-day Israel—he delivers his Sermon on the Mount (5:3–7:27). After this, Jesus continues to teach about the coming of God's "kingdom"—God's direct, manifest reign over everyone and everything (13:1–53). Jesus' vision of God's purposes and Jesus' claim of authority challenge the leaders of Judaism (see chapter 12). Eventually, some of these leaders arrange to have him executed as a political troublemaker (chapters 26–27). At his final meal with his disciples, Jesus reveals that his death will establish a new bond between God and human beings (26:26–29). Soon after his death, to the amazement of his followers, Jesus rises from the dead (chapter 28).

Matthew's Gospel as a whole thus tells of God's decisive action on behalf of men and women through his beloved Son, Jesus. In the Sermon on the Mount, however, Jesus says little about himself or the sweep of God's action through him. The sermon is mainly an invitation to personal transformation. Jesus summons us to make a determined, lifelong effort to model ourselves on the goodwill, kindness, and justice of God. He calls us to reshape our behavior, our speech, and our thinking according to the highest standards of what is right and good.

Taking the sermon to heart requires tremendous effort on our part. But it is crucial to see it as a response to *God's* action. The Gospel as a whole shows that God has taken the initiative. Our action, then, will simply be a response to what God is already doing on our behalf. Jesus precedes his call to personal transformation with the announcement that "the kingdom of heaven has come near" (4:17). His hillside sermon is a part of his ministry of proclaiming and showing that God is bringing people reconciliation and healing (4:23–25). With Jesus' arrival, a new wave of God's action is spreading through human society. Jesus' sermon contains his instructions for how to align ourselves with God's activity, how to live in God's kingdom to the extent that it is already becoming present. Matthew shows that Jesus has accepted a painful death in order to bring us into a new relationship with God (16:21; 26:26–29). It is through this new relationship with God that we find the power to follow the teaching in the sermon.

In the Sermon on the Mount, Jesus urges us to live in a way that fosters justice, peace, harmony, and well-being within and among people. In the rest of his preaching, Jesus makes it clear that God is the one who will ultimately bring about this condition of holiness and wholeness toward which the sermon urges us to strive (see especially his parables—13:1–53). It is God who will abolish every source of sorrow through the final arrival of his kingdom. In the Sermon on the Mount, Jesus provides us with instructions for how to become ready to enter God's kingdom, how to have a place in it when it arrives, how to cooperate with its growth in the world. Yet the coming of God's kingdom—day by day and at the end of time—depends on God's overarching, creative power.

The Sermon on the Mount is not an impersonal lecture. It is an expression of how Jesus approaches life. It reflects his desire for men and women to live in intimacy with God and in peace with one another. Jesus does not depict a distant ideal; rather, he expresses the commitments by which he actually lives—as the rest of the Gospel shows. The sermon offers, in the words of John Paul II, "a sort of self-portrait of Christ." Far from being a mere collection of ethical principles, the sermon conveys Jesus' instructions for how to live as his personal disciples.

Matthew's Gospel presents Jesus as a teacher whose teaching we may accept with complete confidence. Unlike Jesus' original listeners, who did not yet know the outcome of his life, we who read the Gospel know that Jesus willingly endured death in faithfulness to his principles (26:39) and that after dying he entered into risen life with God. Jesus is the teacher of the path to happiness because he has walked the path to its successful conclusion. By his death and resurrection, Jesus went ahead of us on the path, thereby opening it for us.

We will read the Sermon on the Mount section by section. Before we begin, however, it will be useful to get a big-picture view of the sermon as a whole, because its structure helps to express its meaning. Viewed from an altitude of thirty thousand feet, so to speak, the sermon looks like this:

Introduction (5:3–16): Who will be happy?
Beginning (5:17–20): God's law and righteousness
Section 1 (5:21–48): How to interpret God's law
Section 2: PART 1 (6:1–4): Merciful deeds
PART 2 (6:5–15): Prayer
AT THE CENTER (6:9–13): The Lord's Prayer
PART 3 (6:16–18): Fasting
Section 3 (6:19–7:11): On wealth and criticism
End (7:12): God's law is love of neighbor
Conclusion (7:13–27): Choose well!

Notice the placement of the Our Father. The prayer stands out in the middle of the sermon as prominently as a diamond on an engagement ring. This positioning is a clue to the purpose of the sermon: the sermon shows us how to lead a life centered on God. The various instructions in the sermon are pieces of wisdom about how to lead a God-centered life. At the same time, the central placement of the Lord's Prayer suggests that only through personal communion with God our Father can we succeed in following Jesus' instructions.

Equally remarkable is the way that references to God's law in the Old Testament (5:17–20; 7:12) enclose the body of the sermon (5:21–7:11). By framing his teaching in this way, Jesus indicates the continuity of his teaching with God's instructions to Israel through Moses. Jesus is not founding a new religion; he is bringing the religion of Israel to perfection. In addition, the frame highlights the dual principles by which we can discern the core of the Old Testament's ethical heritage: "righteousness" and love of neighbor.

The relationship between Jesus' teaching and the divine commands contained in the Old Testament has been the subject of much debate. How, precisely, does Jesus fulfill the Old Testament commands? This question will confront us especially when we read 5:21–48, where Jesus repeatedly says, "You have heard that it was said. . . . But I say to you . . ."

One explanation of the relationship between the Old Testament commands and Jesus' instructions is that they constitute a lesser and a greater morality. That is to say, Jesus viewed the Mosaic law as deficient and supplied what was lacking. This has been the opinion of some prominent Christian teachers, such as St. Augustine. According to another view, Jesus regarded the Mosaic law as correct but thought that it had become encrusted with misunderstandings—misunderstandings that he pried away.

Whichever view one takes, Jesus' general approach to the Mosaic law in Matthew's Gospel is clear enough. Jesus valued the entire Mosaic law, including its ritual and ceremonial aspects (23:23; 24:20). Matthew never portrays Jesus as speaking against the Mosaic law. Yet among the hundreds of Old Testament precepts, Jesus does focus on those that he believes to be of fundamental importance. He gives primary attention to the Ten Commandments (5:21, 27; 15:1–9) and views rules such as those concerning ritual purity (23:25–26) as relatively minor. Although he does not dismiss any of the Old Testament commands, he has a clear sense of priority: "Woe to you," he tells some religious leaders, "for you tithe mint, dill, and cummin, and have neglected the weightier matters of the law: justice and mercy and faith. It is these you ought to have practiced without neglecting the others" (23:23). Twice in Matthew's Gospel, Jesus quotes an Old Testament oracle in which God declares, "I desire mercy and not sacrifice" (9:13; 12:7; Hosea 6:6). Thus Jesus ranked as first the commands to love God above all and to love one's neighbor as oneself (22:34–40; Deuteronomy 6:5; Leviticus 19:18).

Jesus' disciples were Jews, and Matthew seems to have written for a mainly Jewish-Christian audience. Apparently these Jewish followers of Jesus continued to keep the whole Old Testament law. As Jews, they would have seen the manifold Mosaic law not as an encumbrance but as a gift from God. Consequently, they would have welcomed the gift of Jesus' authoritative interpretation of the law as the guide to following it to perfection. When non-Jews flooded into the Church, however, the question arose of whether they were obliged to keep the ritual requirements of the Mosaic law. Guided by the Holy Spirit, the early Church answered this question with a definite no (Acts 15). For non-Jewish Christians, Jesus' teaching provided not so much a means for interpreting the Mosaic law as the basis for a holy way of life that was free from the ceremonial aspects of the Mosaic law, even while being in continuity with the Mosaic law's fundamental vision of life. This is the value that it has for us today.

The fact that Jesus' disciples and Matthew's first readers were Jewish has an important implication. Jesus' criticisms of religious behavior in the Sermon on the Mount have sometimes been interpreted as criticisms of Jews as Jews—a critique of Judaism. But this cannot be his meaning. Because Jesus, and Matthew, mainly address Jews, the criticisms in the sermon are part of a conversation *among* Jews about the proper way to live as Jews. Take, for example, Jesus' criticism of people who make a show of their acts of charity and their prayers in the synagogue (6:2, 5). This is not, as people have sometimes thought, an attack on the synagogue and on those who attend it; after all, Jesus and his followers belonged to the synagogue (notice that Jesus refers to "the synagogues," not "*their* synagogues"). In targeting hypocrisy in the synagogue, Jesus condemns the fake religiosity that any devout Jew would reject. Jesus' criticisms of defective forms of piety are part of an intra-Jewish, not an anti-Jewish, critique. Thus it is a misuse of the Sermon on the Mount to employ it as an attack on Judaism, either past or present. We who are disciples of Jesus today, whether of Jewish or gentile origin, are likewise subject to the temptation to parade our piety before other people. The sermon is given to us so that we might engage in self-criticism, not criticism of others.

Jesus' sermon calls for careful reading. Jesus speaks in striking metaphors (5:13), in pithy, proverblike exhortations (6:34), in terms sometimes deliberately exaggerated (5:22). His instructions are not to be taken literalistically (in 5:29–30, Jesus does not literally advocate plucking out eyes or amputating hands). His speech is dense, and we must work to unpack his meaning (5:21–48). While Jesus teaches with complete authority, he does not put his instructions in the form of a systematic treatise on ethics; rather, he uses examples, leaving it to us to dig out the underlying principles and determine how they apply to our lives (5:39–42). His words challenge us without telling us precisely what we must do in every specific situation (5:43–48). He calls us not only to new ways of acting but also to new attitudes, even new desires (5:6; 6:19–21). Only if we interact with his words over time, pondering them and trying to act on them, will they shape our minds and hearts.

Jesus' teaching is rich in meaning, allowing for a wealth of interpretations. Through the centuries, saints and scholars have detected ranges of meaning in his words and have come to different conclusions about how they should be applied. Different readers have grasped different aspects of Jesus' message. In a slender book like the present one, it is impossible even to mention all these interpretations. There is space to point out only a few interpretations of the sermon. My selection does not imply that interpretations that are not mentioned are mistaken.

As readers of the Sermon on the Mount, we take our place among the generations of Christians over the centuries who have sought to understand Jesus' words. To each generation making its way through a changing world, Jesus issues his call to a life that is right and good, a life that leads to happiness. Jesus addresses his teaching to each of us as directly as Monsignor Schuler offered his reassurance to each of the high school graduates sitting before him in St. Agnes Church. Jesus challenges you and me to become interpreters of his sermon, seeking to grasp his teaching and apply it to our own particular situations. Then, like St. Agnes herself, depicted in the church ceiling high above the graduates' heads, we will enter the happiness that God has in store for us.

Glossary

Three terms that play an important role in discussing the Sermon on the Mount deserve special attention:

Beatitude. Declaration that someone is happy or is in a situation that will lead to happiness. From a Latin word meaning (could you guess?) "happiness." Examples: 5:3–11 ("Blessed are the poor," etc.).

Torah. Hebrew word meaning "instruction" (see Psalm 32:8, which uses the verbal form of the word: "I will instruct you"). In biblical tradition, *Torah* refers to the first five books of the Bible, which convey God's basic instructions for his people's relationship with him, with one another, and with others. *Torah* is often translated "law" or "the Law," that is, the Mosaic law. Matthew uses the Greek word for *law* to refer to the Torah. It is helpful, however, to keep in mind that *Torah* does not mean "law" in the sense of a criminal code. In the sermon, Jesus indicates that the Torah should not be viewed as a set of legal regulations requiring merely minimal observance but, rather, as a set of instructions on the principles on which we should base our lives. Examples: 5:17; 7:12.

Righteousness. In common usage today, this word has an unpleasant flavor. It suggests an attitude of self-righteousness. Some translations avoid this problem by rendering the underlying Greek word as "justice." But *justice* carries the atmosphere of the courtroom. In biblical tradition, *righteousness* does not have a self-justifying or legalistic connotation. As it is used in the Sermon on the Mount, *righteousness* refers to *God's character* (fairness, mercy, and generosity), to *human actions* (doing what is right, behaving virtuously, acting charitably), and to *a condition of society* (being rightly ordered, having right relationships between people, functioning for the benefit of all its members). Examples: 5:6, 20; 6:33.

Week 1

CONGRATULATIONS!

Questions to Begin

15 minutes
Use a question or two to get warmed up for the reading.

---

1 What's your approach to spices in food?

- ❑ The hotter the better.
- ❑ I'll try anything once.
- ❑ Just pass me the salt.

---

2 Mae West once said, "I've been rich and I've been poor. Believe me, rich is better." What's your opinion?

Opening the Bible

5 minutes
Read the passage aloud. Let individuals take turns reading paragraphs.

The Reading: Psalms 34:6–22; 37:5–11; Matthew 5:1–16

Background: The Psalmists' Faith

Psalm 34:6 This poor soul cried, and was heard by the LORD,
and was saved from every trouble.
7 The angel of the LORD encamps
around those who fear him, and delivers them.
8 O taste and see that the LORD is good;
happy are those who take refuge in him. . . .

15 The eyes of the LORD are on the righteous,
and his ears are open to their cry.
16 The face of the LORD is against evildoers,
to cut off the remembrance of them from the earth.
17 When the righteous cry for help, the LORD hears,
and rescues them from all their troubles.
18 The LORD is near to the brokenhearted,
and saves the crushed in spirit.

19 Many are the afflictions of the righteous,
but the LORD rescues them from them all. . . .
22 The LORD redeems the life of his servants;
none of those who take refuge in him will be
condemned.

37:5 Commit your way to the LORD;
trust in him, and he will act.
6 He will make your vindication shine like the light,
and the justice of your cause like the noonday.

7 Be still before the LORD, and wait patiently for him;
do not fret over those who prosper in their way,
over those who carry out evil devices.

8 Refrain from anger, and forsake wrath.
Do not fret—it leads only to evil.
9 For the wicked shall be cut off,
but those who wait for the LORD shall inherit the
land.

10 Yet a little while, and the wicked will be no more;
though you look diligently for their place, they will not be there.
11 But the meek shall inherit the land,
and delight themselves in abundant prosperity.

Take Your Seat. The Teacher Is About to Begin

Matthew 5:1 When Jesus saw the crowds, he went up the mountain; and
after he sat down, his disciples came to him. 2 Then he began to
speak, and taught them, saying:

3 "Blessed are the poor in spirit, for theirs is the kingdom of heaven.

4 "Blessed are those who mourn, for they will be comforted.

5 "Blessed are the meek, for they will inherit the earth.

6 "Blessed are those who hunger and thirst for righteousness, for they will be filled.

7 "Blessed are the merciful, for they will receive mercy.

8 "Blessed are the pure in heart, for they will see God.

9 "Blessed are the peacemakers, for they will be called children of God.

10 "Blessed are those who are persecuted for righteousness' sake, for theirs is the kingdom of heaven.

11 "Blessed are you when people revile you and persecute
you and utter all kinds of evil against you falsely on my account.
12 Rejoice and be glad, for your reward is great in heaven, for in the
same way they persecuted the prophets who were before you."

You Have a Public Responsibility

13 "You are the salt of the earth; but if salt has lost its taste, how can its saltiness be restored? It is no longer good for anything, but is thrown out and trampled under foot.

14 "You are the light of the world. A city built on a hill
cannot be hid. 15 No one after lighting a lamp puts it under the bushel
basket, but on the lampstand, and it gives light to all in the house.
16 In the same way, let your light shine before others, so that they may
see your good works and give glory to your Father in heaven."

Questions for Careful Reading

10 minutes
Choose questions according to your interest and time.

1 Compare 5:1 with Exodus 34:1–4 (also see Exodus 19:3, 20; 24:15, 18). How are the passages similar? What might be the significance of the similarity?

2 Who are the two groups in Jesus' audience? What different meanings might this first part of the sermon have for each group?

3 The word *meek* is used in 5:5. What does *meek* mean in ordinary usage today? Based on the surrounding statements in 5:3–12, does the modern meaning seem to be what is intended here?

4 Jesus warns his followers that they may encounter persecution. Does he mean this literally? Take a look at Acts 7:54–8:3; 9:1–2.

5 What ordinary uses of salt might Jesus have in mind in 5:13?

A Guide to the Reading

If participants have not read this section already, read it aloud. Otherwise go on to "Questions for Application."

Jesus urges us to view life as a onetime opportunity to journey toward God. He is about to mark out the road to our divine destination (5:17–7:12). Knowing that we will meet with difficulties along the way, he starts with an encouragement: it is good to be on this road, despite its problems and sorrows, because it leads to the ultimate peace and joy—the "kingdom"—for which God has created us (5:3–12).

5:3. Jesus' opening words—"Blessed are the poor in spirit"—serve as a key for unlocking the meaning of all that follows. But who are the "poor in spirit"? And what does it mean that they are "blessed"?

In the Greek text of Matthew's Gospel, the phrase translated "poor in spirit" echoes exactly the phrase translated "crushed in spirit" in the ancient Greek version of Psalm 34:18—an echo of which Matthew must have been aware. Thus we may look to Psalm 34 to help us understand the meaning of poverty of spirit. In that psalm, the "crushed in spirit" are people ground down by the injustices of "evildoers" and by other "afflictions." They are "brokenhearted" because of failure, neediness, and loss. Such people recognize the limitations of the human condition; they know that we cannot "have it all." Yet the crushed in spirit in Psalm 34 trust God in the midst of their neediness; they "take refuge in him" (34:8, 22). Poverty of spirit, then, is the opposite of what we might call "wealth of spirit"; it is the opposite of pride and arrogance. Poverty of spirit guides us toward humility, the vantage point from which we can begin to perceive God. Modern twelve-step programs reflect a certain poverty of spirit: I admit that my behavior has done harm and that I need to change—and that I cannot change without the help of a higher power.

To call the poor in spirit "blessed" is not the same as saying they are happy. People who are crushed in spirit are obviously *not* happy, in the ordinary sense of the term. The beatitude is a striking paradox. In effect, Jesus declares, "Those who lack the blessings of material sufficiency, justice, health, and so on are blessed because they are well positioned to receive greater blessings." To declare the poor in spirit blessed is to congratulate them for being on the right road. They are, we might say, in a good place. Jesus assures them that God will uproot the causes of their present suffering and sorrow when the "kingdom of heaven" comes.

5:4. Those who mourn "will be comforted." Quite simply, mourning is grieving. Those who suffer the death of one deeply loved or loss of health or abandonment by friends or exile from homeland are among "those who mourn." Jesus speaks to all of us who mourn for any reason—because of catastrophes and injustices in the world, because of defects and scandals in the Church, because of our own failures and sins.

Again, "blessed" does not mean "happy." Jesus is not making the absurd assertion that grief is joy. He takes mourning for what it is. *Nevertheless,* he declares, if we are in mourning, we are "blessed," for grief can be the path to great happiness. The beatitude implies that is it better to confront the sorrows of life head-on than to paper over them with artificial cheeriness, with a "happy face" spirituality—or to flee from them into self-destructive behavior. Mourning leads to poverty of spirit, which in turn prepares us to surrender ourselves to God. Then we will be open to being "comforted" by God, who offers us not only sympathetic words but also the promise that he will bring his kingdom.

5:5. Meekness is complex: humility demonstrated in kindness. Jesus alludes to Psalm 37:11: "the meek shall inherit the land." Judging from that psalm, the "meek" are oppressed people who put their lives in God's hands and look forward to the justice that will prevail when his kingdom comes. They hold on to God's hand in the darkness, when terrible events seem to call his power and goodness into question. Meek people do not respond in anger to injury and offense. They do not respond to evil with outbursts of temper (Psalm 37:8) but with patient, constructive action (compare Romans 12:21). In the rest of the sermon, Jesus will dissipate any suspicion that *meek* means "weak." Any man or woman who follows his path of meekness must become a person of strong character indeed.

5:6. Once we have adopted a posture of humility and mourning, we become more aware of the pain of people around us. We begin to notice the injustices that others suffer. Poverty of spirit sensitizes us to the presence in ourselves of the sin that causes so much of the suffering that we decry in the world. When I shake off my pride, for example, I begin to perceive that the kind of hatred that drives terrorists to kill innocent people is present in my own heart—especially toward terrorists. If we are willing, these realizations will give rise to the desire to bring the world, and ourselves, into a better state. This is "hungering and thirsting for righteousness." The desire is twofold: that society as a whole and we ourselves would reflect the righteousness that God intends. It is important to observe that to "hunger and thirst" means both to "long for" and to "make an effort for."

5:7. To be "merciful" is to do merciful deeds and to extend forgiveness. St. Augustine noted that as soon as we try to make progress toward righteousness, we are confronted with our weakness in doing good. We feel the need for God's help. In Augustine's view, Jesus is here suggesting that we express our desire for God's help by giving what help we can to our neighbors. Let us aid our neighbors as generously as we want God to aid us, Augustine recommends; let us forgive them as freely as we want God to forgive us.

5:8. Purity of heart means undivided obedience to God. In the rest of his sermon, Jesus will call us to go beyond merely trying to do the minimum that God requires; he will urge us to make a wholehearted effort to attain the righteousness that God desires—to do what is right not for personal gain but for love of God, to put God's agenda for the world ahead of our own comfort and security. As soon as we try to respond to Jesus' call, difficulties arise, confronting us with the question of whether our primary concern is to serve self or to serve God and others. This is the question of purity of heart.

5:9. Peace is not just an end to fighting; it is society in right order, people sharing God's blessings with one another. God longs for this peace. If we wish to be associated with God, to be his "children," we must share his longing—and we must embrace his means of achieving the goal. As we will see, God's approach to peacemaking in an often warlike world involves great risk-taking and faith.

5:10. The final beatitude ties all eight into a package by repeating the phrase "for theirs is the kingdom of heaven" from verse 3. Thus we are guided to read the beatitudes as a unit: Blessed are those who are poor in spirit *and* mourning *and* meek and so on, because God will give them comfort *and* mercy *and* all his other blessings. The mention of "righteousness" here echoes the fourth beatitude (5:6), thus pointing up righteousness as both the central principle and the final goal. Jesus reveals a God who is totally invested in achieving righteousness—right living, justice—in us and in the world. The recipients of God's blessings will be those who earnestly seek to do what is right in God's eyes and work so that others may enjoy justice.

5:11–12. Without denying that evil causes sadness (recall 5:3–4), Jesus declares that even in painful situations we can experience the joy of knowing that God's kingdom will prevail over every form of evil (see Romans 5:3–5).

Looking back over the beatitudes, I am astonished by their challenge. Jesus summons me to overcome my deep-rooted egotism. How much I need to change in order to be the kind of person Jesus congratulates! He comforts me with the assurance of a kingdom that, to my secularized eyes, often seems ethereal and distant. How much I need to change in order to feel encouraged by the assurance that Jesus offers!

5:13–16. Jesus makes it clear that his is not a merely private spirituality. He calls us to a mission to the world, for the world. The beatitudes are not merely a formula for achieving personal aspirations or forming relationships within the Christian community. Jesus invites us to act in the midst of a world that is suffering poverty and grief and hoping for justice and peace. (For additional discussion, see "Between Discussions," page 26.)

Questions for Application

40 minutes
Choose questions according to your interest and time.

1. Where in your life—or in the lives of people you know—has the lack of material blessings prepared the way for receiving greater blessings?

2. What is the difference between being poor in spirit and giving up on yourself or on life—or even on God? How do the poor in spirit respond to hardship? Is there a situation in your life where you need to respond in this way?

3. Does anything in this reading stand out as new, inspiring, or challenging to you? As you read 5:3–10, which beatitude stands out most prominently? What might God wish to say to you through this beatitude? What step could you take to respond?

4. Persecution may take various forms. What forms does it take in contemporary society? Have you had any experience of this? If so, what have you learned from it?

5 What suggestions and cautions can you offer with regard to using the beatitudes to console or encourage someone? Given the differences between the beatitudes, it may be best to consider each one separately.

6 What does it mean to be salt and light for the people you interact with every day? How could you grow in being salt and light for them?

7 How can we express love and care for people in a way that allows them to see our good works and also helps them recognize that the source of our good works is our Father in heaven?

Our Bible journey can be more fun if we encourage other seekers to accompany us. . . . Talking with others also provides a good sounding board for testing our impressions and conclusions.

Steve Mueller, *The Seeker's Guide to Reading the Bible*

Approach to Prayer

15 minutes
Use one of these approaches—or create your own!

- Pray either Psalm 34 or Psalm 37:1–11. Provide an opportunity for silent or spontaneous prayers. Conclude with an Our Father.

- Use the beatitudes as your prayer. Ask one person to read 5:3–10 out loud, pausing after each verse to allow the group to pray, "Make us your people, Lord." Then spend a couple of minutes in silent reflection. Conclude with an Our Father.

1 | *Psalms 34:6–22; 37:5–11; Matthew 5:1–16*

Saints in the Making

A Young Man of the Beatitudes

This section is a supplement for individual reading.

When Pier Giorgio Frassati was quite small, his grandfather took him to visit a nursery school. At lunchtime, Pier Giorgio quickly noticed one boy, whose face was marred by a skin disease, eating apart from the others. Pier Giorgio immediately seated himself next to the boy and shared his lunch. As a young teen, Pier Giorgio kept a notebook containing the names and addresses of impoverished families he met. He would duck out of recreational activities to bring them small gifts.

By the time he was in college, in the early 1920s, Pier Giorgio's aid to his suffering fellow citizens in Turin, Italy, had become systematic. He regularly visited residents of a hospital for the mentally and physically disabled, bringing them candy, clothing, and cheerful conversation. He worked with the St. Vincent de Paul Society, calling on needy families and securing various kinds of assistance for them. Pier Giorgio considered becoming a priest but rejected the idea, because he thought he could have a closer relationship with working-class people as a layman. So he studied engineering and planned a career in mining—a field where he would be surrounded by workers in blue collars. Despite his family's wealth—his father was a prominent newspaper publisher and an Italian ambassador to Germany—Pier Giorgio had only a small allowance. But he preferred to travel third-class rather than first-class on trains and to share the savings with others.

Frassati's mother was a not very devout Catholic; his father was an agnostic. Pier Giorgio's life was a tightrope walk between his parents' expectations for his success and his desire to escape his privileged lifestyle and live as an ordinary person, dedicating his energies to serving people in need. His tightrope walk ended at age twenty-four, when he died from polio.

Frassati died in 1925. In the following decade, his life inspired a young Polish student, Karol Wojtyla. In 1990, Wojtyla—as Pope John Paul II—declared Frassati "blessed," a step toward sainthood. Calling Frassati "a man of the eight Beatitudes," the pope has said that Pier Giorgio "proclaims that a life lived in the Spirit of the Beatitudes is 'blessed,' and that only the person who becomes a 'man or woman of the Beatitudes' can succeed in communicating love and peace to others."

Between Discussions

The portion of Jesus' sermon that we have just read is so rich in meaning that we will pause here to look back and reflect on it some more. Next session's portion also contains much to explore, so we will get started on it in this section.

Looking back. Jesus concludes his beatitudes by referring to the opposition that we are likely to encounter if we live the way he recommends (5:10–12). He may still be thinking about opposition as he goes on to speak about the public nature of our role (5:13–16), for he warns us not to compromise the qualities that make us distinctive as his followers. Rather, we should let our merciful actions, our commitment to justice and peace, be visible in the world.

Jesus makes his point by combining ordinary images in surprising ways. There was nothing unusual about ceramic oil lamps. But the idea of putting a burning lamp under a wicker basket is not only ridiculous but also alarming. Salt has a variety of uses, and commentators have discussed which use Jesus has in mind here. The most common use of salt, and thus the most likely reference, is to flavor food. As the most basic seasoning, salt is necessary and irreplaceable. Jesus' point, then, is that his followers serve a necessary and irreplaceable function in the world. The qualities that make us "salty" are meekness, mercy, peacemaking, and so on—those things he has just mentioned in the beatitudes. The uniqueness of our role in the world is suggested by his declaration that we are "the" salt of the earth. Jesus assigns to his followers a mission that no other body of people in the world can carry out.

Salt seasons food by being mixed into it—not by staying in a box. The image of salt, then, suggests that our mission involves mingling with other people. While periods of solitude are essential for spiritual life (6:6)—and while some men and women are called to a life of prayer in monasteries and convents far from the mainstream of society—the Church as a whole has a role to play at the center of the world. New Testament scholar Hans Dieter Betz makes this observation on Jesus' image of his disciples as salt: "The faithful disciples must get involved with this earth and its life. . . . There can be no doubt that this means a life under hazardous conditions. One might refer to another proverbial image: 'Behold, I send you as sheep in the midst of wolves' (Matthew 10:16). Yet, the life of the faithful disciples is not that of passive and helpless victims, but that of movers and shakers: it is a life of 'doers.' Every single situation described in the Sermon on the Mount puts the disciples into the center of trouble, difficulties, and hard choices. This is the place where they must 'seek the kingdom of God and his righteousness' (Matthew 6:33)."

The image of the burning oil lamp (5:14–16) helps to explain the nature of our role. We are to let our light shine out so that other people may see our good works and "give glory" to our Father in heaven (5:16). Clearly, the light we are supposed to show to people is, in origin, *God's* light, since others will praise God, not us, when they see it. The "good works" are the sort of deeds that God does—showing mercy, establishing justice, making peace. The virtues that Jesus identifies in the beatitudes are the qualities of God. If we become men and women of the beatitudes, people who look at us will catch a glimpse of God—and will thank him for his goodness.

Notice that *light* is singular. Yet in the Greek, the words translated "you" and "your" in 5:14–16 are plural. Jesus is not speaking of many individual lights. He is saying, "The group of you is the light." It is by working together as Jesus' followers that we will reflect the presence of our heavenly Father in the world.

Looking ahead. "Do not think that I have come to abolish the law . . ." (5:17–20). In the section of Jesus' sermon that we are about to read, he will make six on-the-contrary statements, each drawing a contrast between what people have heard about God's will and Jesus' own position (5:21–48). Is Jesus retiring the Old Testament commands and replacing them with his own expression of God's will? At first glance, Jesus may seem to be disagreeing with God's commands in the Old Testament. But Jesus warns us at the outset to avoid this impression (5:17). His approach to the Torah is complex and subtle; it should not be misunderstood as rejection. He does not take issue with the Torah itself but with interpretations that obscure its meaning. He seeks to dispose of these misinterpretations of God's will.

"I have come not to abolish but to fulfill," Jesus announces (5:17). He intends to show us how to carry out God's commands in a way that fulfills their purpose. One way of expressing the purpose of God's commands is "righteousness" (5:20), that is, being just and merciful in imitation of God, living in a way that fosters justice and peace among people (5:44–45, 48). Individual divine commands show us how to progress toward this goal. Another way of stating the purpose of God's commands is to say that they instruct us in how to best serve our neighbor's welfare. Jesus declares that God's law is fulfilled when we treat others as we would like to be treated (7:12; compare 22:34–40). God's law comes into focus when we view it through the lens of this Golden Rule. Thus the way to properly interpret and apply God's commands is to ask questions such as "What does this teaching show me about how to foster what is right and just?" and "How does this instruction guide me in loving my neighbor?"

In his six "antitheses"—statements of contrast—Jesus rejects interpretations of God's commands that arise from viewing them mainly as civil and criminal laws. Legal scholar Benjamin Cardozo defined *law* as "the sum total of community morality that judges deem it expedient and practicable to uphold by the use of force." Civil and criminal laws, then, merely specify the minimum we must do to avoid penalties. In Jesus' view, God's commands in the Torah are not essentially legal limits on our behavior, such as can be enforced by the state. Rather, God's commands are what the Hebrew word *Torah* basically means: "instruction." They instruct us in how to achieve righteousness. That is, the divine commands show us how to relate to friends, strangers, members of the opposite sex, and enemies so as to achieve God's goal of harmony among human beings. Jesus does not deny that God's commands may also provide elements to undergird a legal system. But this is not a subject that he explores in the Sermon on the Mount. Rather, he emphasizes that the primary purpose of God's commands is to convey God's vision for human life.

Thus Jesus insists that we not approach God's commands in a legalistic way, as minimal standards of behavior. Loving children do not aim at merely doing the minimum that their parents require. Similarly, God's sons and daughters should try to grasp what their Father is aiming at through his commands and should put their energies into attaining his goals. In his six antitheses, Jesus will give examples of how to apply this approach to God's commands. He trains us to ask, "What is the summons to justice and love that God is giving me through this or that divine command?"

Jesus' on-the-contrary statements take a specific form. First, he quotes or paraphrases Scripture. Second, he cites an erroneous interpretation drawn from an oral tradition (5:43) or an application within Scripture itself that is open to misunderstanding (5:21, 33), or he simply lets the Scripture quotation stand without further interpretation (5:27, 31, 38). In the latter case, he implicitly takes issue with the *apparent* meaning of the command. In other words, he regards the literalistic interpretation of the command as mistaken. Third, he presents his own interpretation, bringing to light the fundamental intention of the scriptural command.

Before moving on, it would be instructive to take another look at 5:22: "But I say to you . . ." Who is this man who speaks with such authority about God's will for human beings? He claims to know God's will so well that he can confidently identify the original purpose of God's commands—and can speak with assurance about the ultimate consequences of failing to achieve God's purpose. One scholar comments that while Jesus interprets God's law as it was revealed in the Old Testament, he does so not as its servant but as its Lord.

Week 2

DON'T BE A MINIMALIST

Questions to Begin

15 minutes
Use a question or two to get warmed up for the reading.

---

1 When you were growing up, what was your approach to work such as chores and homework?

- ❑ How can I get out of this?
- ❑ What's the absolute minimum that has to be done?
- ❑ I'll do my best.
- ❑ Let me at it!

---

2 Describe a situation in your life in which someone was intensely concerned about rules and regulations being followed to the letter. Was their (or your) approach justified?

Opening the Bible

5 minutes
Read the passage aloud. Let individuals take turns reading paragraphs.

The Reading: Matthew 5:17–32; 19:3–9

Please Don't Misunderstand

17 “Do not think that I have come to abolish the law or the prophets;
I have come not to abolish but to fulfill. 18 For truly I tell you, until
heaven and earth pass away, not one letter, not one stroke of a letter,
will pass from the law until all is accomplished. 19 Therefore, whoever
breaks one of the least of these commandments, and teaches others to
do the same, will be called least in the kingdom of heaven; but
whoever does them and teaches them will be called great in the
kingdom of heaven. 20 For I tell you, unless your righteousness
exceeds that of the scribes and Pharisees, you will never enter the
kingdom of heaven.”

Grasp God's Purpose

21 “You have heard that it was said to those of ancient times, ‘You
shall not murder’; and ‘whoever murders shall be liable to judgment.’
22 But I say to you that if you are angry with a brother or sister, you
will be liable to judgment; and if you insult a brother or sister, you will
be liable to the council; and if you say, ‘You fool,’ you will be liable to
the hell of fire. 23 So when you are offering your gift at the altar, if you
remember that your brother or sister has something against you,
24 leave your gift there before the altar and go; first be reconciled to
your brother or sister, and then come and offer your gift. 25 Come to
terms quickly with your accuser while you are on the way to court
with him, or your accuser may hand you over to the judge, and the
judge to the guard, and you will be thrown into prison. 26 Truly I tell
you, you will never get out until you have paid the last penny.”

Two Other Examples

27 “You have heard that it was said, ‘You shall not commit adultery.’
28 But I say to you that everyone who looks at a woman with lust has
already committed adultery with her in his heart. 29 If your right eye
causes you to sin, tear it out and throw it away; it is better for you to
lose one of your members than for your whole body to be thrown
into hell. 30 And if your right hand causes you to sin, cut it off and

throw it away; it is better for you to lose one of your members than
for your whole body to go into hell.
31 "It was also said, 'Whoever divorces his wife, let him give
her a certificate of divorce.' 32 But I say to you that anyone who
divorces his wife, except on the ground of unchastity, causes her to
commit adultery; and whoever marries a divorced woman commits
adultery."

A Later Statement by Jesus

19:3 Some Pharisees came to him, and to test him they asked, "Is it
lawful for a man to divorce his wife for any cause?" 4 He answered,
"Have you not read that the one who made them at the beginning
'made them male and female,' 5 and said, 'For this reason a man
shall leave his father and mother and be joined to his wife, and the
two shall become one flesh'? 6 So they are no longer two, but one
flesh. Therefore what God has joined together, let no one separate."
7 They said to him, "Why then did Moses command us to give a
certificate of dismissal and to divorce her?" 8 He said to them, "It
was because you were so hard-hearted that Moses allowed you to
divorce your wives, but from the beginning it was not so. 9 And I say
to you, whoever divorces his wife, except for unchastity, and marries
another commits adultery."

Questions for Careful Reading

10 minutes
Choose questions according to your interest and time.

1 What does 5:17 suggest about some people's impression of Jesus' teaching?

2 Reread 5:19. Do Jesus' words imply that there might be different ranks in heaven? Consider also 11:11; 18:1–4; 20:21–23.

3 When Jesus says "but" in 5:22 and 5:28, is he disagreeing entirely with the preceding statements?

4 What similarities are there between the first two anitheses (5:21–26 and 5:27–30)?

5 Which of Jesus' statements in this reading seem meant to be taken literally? Which statements seem not intended to be taken literally?

A Guide to the Reading

If participants have not read this section already, read it aloud. Otherwise go on to "Questions for Application."

5:21–26. "You shall not murder": Jesus is quoting the Ten Commandments (Exodus 20:13). What follows—"whoever murders shall be liable to judgment"—is a stipulation of criminal law that appears elsewhere in Scripture in various forms (Exodus 21:12; Leviticus 24:17). Jesus disagrees with something about these statements. What exactly does he disagree with?

The statement "whoever murders shall be liable to judgment" treats "you shall not murder" as a criminal law. Society certainly needs criminal laws. Criminal laws define behavior that must be avoided. But God does not give his commands merely in order to forbid certain gross types of evil. He gives his commands in order to communicate his vision for how humans ought to relate to one another. To interpret God's commands properly, we should not ask legal questions such as "What do I have to avoid?" or "What is the minimum I have to do?" Rather, we should ask ethical questions: "What 'good' or value, what aspect of 'righteousness,' does God seek to foster through this command? How can I best achieve that good?"

Killing is the ultimate breakdown in relations between persons. By forbidding killing, God conveys the importance he places on just, harmonious relations between people. "You shall not murder" implies that we should curb whatever leads to the disruption of our relationships with one another. If we are serious about attaining harmony with other people, we will come to grips with the anger that poisons our dealings with others and drives us to harm them (5:22; compare Psalm 37:8, which says literally, "Do not fly into a passion, for it leads to doing evil").

"If you say, 'You fool,' you will be liable to the hell of fire" (5:22). Jesus conveys his teaching through sharp, sometimes exaggerated examples aimed at jolting us into a new way of seeing. We must interpret his words as he himself interprets the Torah, by grasping the purpose. Here he is trying to get us to see that we must put aside everything, even words, *even desires,* that aim at hurting other people. It does not seem, however, that he is declaring that all angry feelings or reproachful words are harmful. Jesus himself grew angry on occasion and rebuked those who committed injustices (see chapter 23).

The command "you shall not murder" points to the importance not only of protecting existing personal relationships but also of repairing relationships already ruptured by wrongdoing. Reconciliation is so important that it takes priority over religious actions such as (in Jesus' day) making offerings in the Jerusalem temple (5:23–24). Offerings to God are supposed to express love for God, and love for God must be expressed in love for neighbor; therefore it makes no sense to bring offerings to God if we have not sought forgiveness from people we have injured.

Jesus' statement about leaving your sacrifice at the altar until you are reconciled with your neighbor is obviously an example, not a rule. As St. Augustine observed, how could we do this for a brother or sister who lives across the sea? In such a case, Augustine thought, we should humble ourselves before the absent brother or sister in prayer, thus preparing ourselves to ask their pardon when we see them again. Of course, Augustine lived before phones and e-mail.

Jesus' counsel to avoid lawsuits (5:25–26) is inspired common sense. Lawsuits are risky. We are well advised to put aside rage and become (as 5:25 says literally) "well-disposed" toward our adversary. Adopting an attitude of friendliness toward our opponent does not guarantee that he or she will come around to a better attitude toward us. But such an approach puts the brakes on an accelerating conflict and creates an opportunity for reconciliation.

5:27–32. "But I say to you . . ." Obviously, Jesus is not disagreeing with the command to avoid adultery! "Yes, but . . ." would catch his sense. On the face of it, "you shall not commit adultery" may seem to mean simply that the physical act of adultery is forbidden, but Jesus disagrees with such a literalistic interpretation. Like "you shall not murder," the command "you shall not commit adultery" should not be treated as a legal minimum, a mere basis for criminal law. The command against adultery instructs us in the importance that God places on marriage. Again, once we have grasped the good, or value, that the command fosters, we see that we must take control of our sexual desire and adjust our behavior so as to avoid violating this value (5:27–30).

Questions for Application

40 minutes
Choose questions according to your interest and time.

1. Can you think of instances in which a person might be scrupulous about observing a rule without taking into account the purpose of the rule?

2. When have you seen or experienced the damage that angry words can cause? What have these situations taught you about probing the causes of your own anger and dealing constructively with situations that make you angry? Where do you need to grow in dealing constructively with such a situation in your present life?

3. What practical steps can a man or a woman take to implement Jesus' teaching in 5:28?

4. What could you do to deepen your understanding and appreciation of marriage? What could you do to strengthen your own marriage or the marriages of others?

5 What dangers might lie in interpreting Jesus' figures of speech in this reading in a literalistic way?

6 For personal reflection: Who are the people in your life who seem to bear you ill will or do things that seem to be against your best interests? What guidance for dealing with these people can you find in Jesus' words in 5:22? What do you need to guard against in the way you think and speak about these people? How might you foster peace with them?

Team learning . . . calls for shared responsibility. . . . You cannot expect to learn from one another until you first do some discovering yourself.

Oletta Wald, *The Joy of Discovery*

Approach to Prayer

15 minutes
Use this approach—or create your own!

- Use the Ten Commandments as a checklist to examine privately your thoughts, speech, and behavior. Let participants take turns reading the following verses one at a time, pausing after each one for silent reflection: Exodus 20:2–3, 7, 8, 12, 13, 14, 15, 16, 17. Then pray Psalm 51, letting participants take turns reading the verses. Close with an Our Father.

A Living Tradition

The Decalogue

This section is a supplement for individual reading.

Christian catechisms have often used the Ten Commandments as an outline for moral instruction. The current *Catechism of the Catholic Church* speaks at length on the commandments. Here are excerpts from the Catechism's discussion (sections 2056–2063).

The word "Decalogue" means literally "ten words."[1] God revealed these "ten words" to his people on the holy mountain. They were written "with the finger of God,"[2] unlike the other commandments written by Moses.[3] They are pre-eminently the words of God. . . .

The Decalogue must first be understood in the context of the Exodus, God's great liberating event at the center of the Old Covenant. Whether formulated as negative commandments, prohibitions, or as positive precepts such as: "Honor your father and mother," the "ten words" point out the conditions of a life freed from the slavery of sin. The Decalogue is a path of life. . . .

The Commandments take on their full meaning within the covenant. According to Scripture, man's moral life has all its meaning in and through the covenant. The first of the "ten words" recalls that God loved his people first:

"Since there was a passing from the paradise of freedom to the slavery of this world, in punishment for sin, the first phrase of the Decalogue, the first word of God's commandments, bears on freedom: 'I am the LORD your God, who brought you out of the land of Egypt, out of the house of slavery.'"[4]

The Commandments properly so-called come in the second place: they express the implications of belonging to God through the establishment of the covenant. Moral existence is a *response* to the Lord's loving initiative. It is the acknowledgement and homage given to God and a worship of thanksgiving. It is cooperation with the plan God pursues in history.

1. Exodus 34:28; Deuteronomy 4:13; 10:4.
2. Exodus 31:18; Deuteronomy 5:22.
3. Compare Deuteronomy 31:9, 24.
4. Origen, *Homilies on Exodus* 8, 1: *Patrologia Graeca* 12, 350; compare Exodus 20:2; Deuteronomy 5:6.

Between Discussions

Jesus' teaching on divorce (5:31–32) touches on a subject so close to home for many of us that it deserves special attention. To start with, it is helpful to see that Jesus' teaching on divorce is connected to his teaching on sexual desires outside marriage (5:27–30). The good, or value, at stake in the command "you shall not commit adultery" is the unity between husband and wife. A person who grasps this value will try to avoid anything that disrupts the marriage relationship. He or she will curb the erotic desires that would lead to adultery and any behavior that would undermine marriage. Jesus' words about adultery, sexual desires, and divorce are couched in negative terms, but they have a positive purpose: to help us to recognize how important marriage is in God's eyes and to commit ourselves to doing what we can to strengthen marriages—including our own.

Jesus gives a paraphrase of a passage from Deuteronomy: "Whoever divorces his wife, let him give her a certificate of divorce" (5:31; Deuteronomy 24:1–4). On the face of it, this Old Testament passage permits divorce and remarriage under certain circumstances. But Jesus disagrees with something in this passage ("But I say to you . . ." [5:32]). It may be that Jesus views the Deuteronomy passage as a concession that is now withdrawn. Some Old Testament precepts limit certain evils without eliminating them. For example, "an eye for an eye" limits compensation for an injury without eliminating the hatred felt by the injured party (5:38–42). The fact that a law reduces an evil without doing away with it does not imply that the lawmaker gives the behavior in question a stamp of approval. Consider an analogy from family life: a mother might forbid her daughter to see R-rated movies but allow her to see movies rated PG-13. It is not that the mother thinks PG-13 movies are problem free. She may simply fear that a stricter rule would do more harm than good by leading to ceaseless conflict with her daughter. This kind of situation seems to arise in the Torah regarding divorce. Various stipulations seem to have been designed to regularize, and thus limit, divorce (Deuteronomy 22:13–19, 28–29 and perhaps the passage that Jesus cites—Deuteronomy 24:1–4).

Jesus' approach to the Torah is to seek out the vision of righteousness that God expressed by his commands. Thus the principles that underlie the Torah remain, but those precepts that sought only to reduce wrongdoing, rather than eliminate it, pass away. Later in Matthew's Gospel, Jesus declares that the time has come to put aside the Mosaic concession to the human tendencies that lead to divorce; his followers should now pursue God's original intention of unity between spouses (19:1–9; Genesis 1:27 and 2:24). Jesus' approach is not an overturning of the Mosaic law, because withdrawing a concession does not imply a change of principle. The Torah never declared that divorce was good. Similarly, if the mother decided to make PG-13 movies also off-limits to her daughter, she would not be reversing her previous policy of moral guidance but simply making it more consistent.

What about "except on the ground of unchastity"? One explanation that has been proposed is as follows: "unchastity" here refers to sexual activity outside of marriage, thus in the present discussion, adultery. Jesus' reasoning may be that if a man divorces his wife, he puts her in the situation of needing to marry someone else. But since the first marriage still stands in God's eyes, her second marriage is a kind of adultery. However, if a wife has committed adultery (therefore becoming "unchaste"), divorcing her will not put her in the situation of committing adultery, for she has committed adultery already. Thus, it is permissible for the husband to divorce her. Indeed, in the Jewish culture of the time, a husband might feel obliged to separate from his wife if she committed adultery. We see this approach in the case of Joseph, who felt that he ought to separate from Mary, his betrothed, because he thought she had slept with another man (1:18–19). While Jesus seems to allow that a husband might divorce his wife if she has already ruptured the marriage by committing adultery, he does not say that either spouse would then be free to marry someone else. In fact, Jesus' position against remarriage after divorce is one of the most widely attested aspects of his teaching (19:1–9; Mark 10:1–12; Luke 16:18; 1 Corinthians 7:10–11).

The discussion in Matthew deals with divorce from the husband's point of view, as was the custom in Jewish discussions at the time. But see Mark 10:11–12. For a discussion of the Catholic understanding of marriage, divorce, and remarriage, see the *Catechism of the Catholic Church*, sections 2360–2385.

Week 3

Be Like Your Father

Questions to Begin

15 minutes
Use a question or two to get warmed up for the reading.

---

1 When have you told the truth even though it was hard to do so?

---

2 What habit, preference, or mannerism have you picked up from your father? from your mother?

Opening the Bible

5 minutes
Read the passage aloud. Let individuals take turns reading paragraphs.

The Reading: Leviticus 19:13–18; Matthew 5:33–48; 22:34–40

Background: The Torah on Love and Hate

Leviticus 19:13 You shall not defraud your neighbor; you shall not steal;
and you shall not keep for yourself the wages of a laborer until
morning. 14 You shall not revile the deaf or put a stumbling block
before the blind; you shall fear your God: I am the LORD.

15 You shall not render an unjust judgment; you shall not be
partial to the poor or defer to the great: with justice you shall judge
your neighbor. 16 You shall not go around as a slanderer among your
people, and you shall not profit by the blood of your neighbor: I am
the LORD.

17 You shall not hate in your heart anyone of your kin; you
shall reprove your neighbor, or you will incur guilt yourself. 18 You
shall not take vengeance or bear a grudge against any of your people,
but you shall love your neighbor as yourself: I am the LORD.

Just Tell the Truth

Matthew 5:33 "Again, you have heard that it was said to those of ancient
times, 'You shall not swear falsely, but carry out the vows you have
made to the Lord.' 34 But I say to you, Do not swear at all, either by
heaven, for it is the throne of God, 35 or by the earth, for it is his
footstool, or by Jerusalem, for it is the city of the great King. 36 And
do not swear by your head, for you cannot make one hair white or
black. 37 Let your word be 'Yes, Yes' or 'No, No'; anything more than
this comes from the evil one."

Love As God Loves

38 "You have heard that it was said, 'An eye for an eye and a tooth
for a tooth.' 39 But I say to you, Do not resist an evildoer. But if
anyone strikes you on the right cheek, turn the other also; 40 and if
anyone wants to sue you and take your coat, give your cloak as well;
41 and if anyone forces you to go one mile, go also the second mile.
42 Give to everyone who begs from you, and do not refuse anyone
who wants to borrow from you.

43 "You have heard that it was said, 'You shall love your
neighbor and hate your enemy.' 44 But I say to you, Love your
enemies and pray for those who persecute you, 45 so that you may be
children of your Father in heaven; for he makes his sun rise on the
evil and on the good, and sends rain on the righteous and on the
unrighteous. 46 For if you love those who love you, what reward do
you have? Do not even the tax collectors do the same? 47 And if you
greet only your brothers and sisters, what more are you doing than
others? Do not even the Gentiles do the same? 48 Be perfect, therefore,
as your heavenly Father is perfect."

A Later Statement by Jesus

22:34 When the Pharisees heard that he had silenced the Sadducees,
they gathered together, 35 and one of them, a lawyer, asked him a
question to test him. 36 "Teacher, which commandment in the law is
the greatest?" 37 He said to him, "'You shall love the Lord your God
with all your heart, and with all your soul, and with all your mind.'
38 This is the greatest and first commandment. 39 And a second is like
it: 'You shall love your neighbor as yourself.' 40 On these two
commandments hang all the law and the prophets."

Questions for Careful Reading

10 minutes
Instead of separate questions to help you probe the text, here is an exercise.

---

1 Jesus gives six examples of how to interpret God's Old Testament commands. He co have given additional examples For instance, we can imagine Jesus saying, "You have heard that it was said to those of ancient times, 'You shall not steal,' and 'When someone steals an ox, the thief shall pay five oxen for an ox.' But I say to you . . ." (see Exodus 20:15; 22:1). How would you complete this example? What positive values lie behind these two Old Testament precepts? What would wholehearted commitment to these values look like in everyday life?

---

2 How would you apply Jesus' reasoning to Leviticus 19:16: "You shall not go around as a slanderer among your people"? Try applying Jesus' reasoning to the precepts in these verses: Exodus 21:15, Exodus 21:16, Exodus 21:33–34, Exodus 22:6, Leviticus 19:32.

A Guide to the Reading

If participants have not read this section already, read it aloud. Otherwise go on to "Questions for Application."

5:33–37. The Old Testament contains instructions about swearing truthfully and fulfilling vows (Leviticus 19:12; Deuteronomy 23:21–23). These instructions were meant to move people toward integrity in speech. Jesus calls us to embrace this purpose. Commit yourself to making all your statements true and to carrying out all your promises, he says. You don't need to take an oath to signal that you're speaking the truth.

5:38–42. "You have heard that it was said, 'An eye for an eye and a tooth for a tooth.' But I say to you, Do not resist an evildoer . . ." Despite Jesus' announcement that he has come "not to abolish but to fulfill" (5:17), here he certainly *seems* to be overturning Old Testament law. But let us look more closely.

In his treatment of adultery (5:27–28) Jesus upheld the command ("you shall not commit adultery") but disagreed with the seemingly obvious interpretation (*just* avoid the physical act of adultery). Likewise, here Jesus objects to the seemingly obvious interpretation of "an eye for an eye." On the face of it, "an eye for an eye" set a requirement: every wrong must be counterbalanced with an equal punishment. Not so! Jesus declares. The command did not *insist* on punishment but limited it. Punishment must never exceed the original wrong: *only* "an eye for an eye" (contrast Lamech's statements in Genesis 4:23–24). Furthermore, "an eye for an eye" shifted the response to injury from retaliation to adjudication; it moved conflict from the back alley to the courtroom, where those who were wronged might seek redress within a legal framework rather than in endless feuding. Thus "an eye for an eye" was a step toward reconciliation and peace. Jesus now urges us to perceive this purpose behind the command and to strive for it. Act even more decisively to break the cycle of violence and retaliation, Jesus says—don't even seek an eye for an eye.

"Do not resist an evildoer" might better be translated "Do not retaliate." Jesus does not mean that we should passively step aside and let evildoers go from bad to worse. No one who hungers and thirsts for righteousness could do that. Rather, we should use our willingness to suffer injury to redirect people from evil toward good. Regarding Jesus' counsel to turn the other cheek, Hans Dieter Betz writes: "The gesture exposes the act of the offender as what it is: morally repulsive. . . . It challenges the striker to react with comparable generosity."

5:43–48. "You shall love your neighbor and hate your enemy." The NRSV places this whole statement in quotation marks as a citation from the Torah. But only "you shall love your neighbor" comes from the Torah (Leviticus 19:18); "hate your enemy" is an extension added by popular understanding that gives the command a certain interpretation. Jesus supports the Torah command but disagrees strongly with the popular interpretation.

The command "you shall love your neighbor" might be taken to mean that we should make our neighbors—that is, our friends—the object of our love. The corollary would be that we should not love the rest of the world, and certainly not people who harm us. Indeed, this is how the command was interpreted in popular tradition; people considered it normal to love their neighbor and hate their enemy (see 2 Samuel 19:5–6). Jesus rejects this interpretation, *since all our fellow human beings are our neighbors.* Thus the command to love our neighbor does not limit our favor to our families and friends; rather, it directs us toward a universal love, a love for every human being. This was the lesson of Jesus' parable about the Samaritan who helped an injured traveler (Luke 10:29–37). If everyone is included in the notion of "neighbor," then even those who seek to harm us are our neighbors. Consequently, even they are to be loved.

Earlier Jesus spoke of peacemakers (5:9). Now we see what is involved in peacemaking, Jesus-style. Peacemaking does not mean having nice feelings toward irritating people. Peacemakers are those who do good to those who do them harm. In the end, Jesus' teaching about loving one's enemies is quite simple—although almost impossible to put into practice!

Jesus bases his call to universal love on God's behavior (5:44–45). God blesses the good and the bad. Does this seem unjust? In Jesus' view, generosity and mercy are not opposed to justice—they are part of it. Notice that he does not promise that our love will make our enemies into friends. The bedrock reason for this course of action is not the response that might come of it but our duty to imitate our Father.

Questions for Application

40 minutes
Choose questions according to your interest and time.

1 Have you ever made a promise to God? Why? What happened? What did you learn from this experience?

2 Have you ever needed forgiveness from someone and received it abundantly—or been denied? How did this affect you? Who needs your forgiveness?

3 Do you know of anyone who wishes to do you harm? How might Jesus' teaching in this reading guide you in dealing with this person?

4 Augustine wrote that peacemakers are those who are at peace with God. His reasoning is as follows: only those at peace with God will have God's grace to put their emotions under the rule of their reason. Only those who live by reason rather than emotion are at peace within themselves. Only those who are at peace within themselves can work effectively for peace among others in the manner that Jesus teaches (5:21–26, 38–48). What do you think of Augustine's reasoning?

5 Considering the great efforts to which Jesus calls us—dealing severely with ourselves regarding sexual temptations, being faithful in marriage even when there are heavy burdens, being truthful in all circumstances—Augustine notes that only a person who hungers and thirsts for righteousness (5:6) would accept these challenging commands. What other connections can you detect between Jesus' teaching in 5:21–48 and the beatitudes?

6 What do Jesus' words in 5:38–48 mean for the exercise of force by the government? for the use of war to deal with international problems? (These are long-debated issues! Consider the *Catechism of the Catholic Church,* sections 2303–2317.)

Reading scripture is important for the life of every Christian, particularly for those who are required to make difficult decisions. . . . The word of God is . . . a source of discernment and sensitivity regarding the signs of the Holy Spirit in our situation.

Cardinal Carlo Martini, Catholic biblical scholar and archbishop of Milan, Italy

Approach to Prayer

15 minutes
Use this approach—or create your own!

- Allow participants an opportunity to voice prayers of intercession for the needs of neighbors and prayers asking for God's help to be peacemakers. Spend a few minutes in silence, then close with an Our Father.

3 | *Leviticus 19:13–18; Matthew 5:33–48; 22:34–40*

Saints in the Making

Not "An Eye for an Eye"

This section is a supplement for individual reading.

Julie Welch, a Spanish translator for the Social Security Administration, was one of the people who died in the bombing of the Federal Building in Oklahoma City in 1995. She was twenty-three years old. Four years later, her father, Bud Welch, offered remarks on the death penalty to an audience at Harvard University.

All my life, I had always opposed the death penalty. My entire family has, even going back to my grandparents. . . . Well, after Tim McVeigh bombed the Oklahoma City Federal Building, the rage, the hate—you can't think of enough words to describe what I felt. I did change my mind about the death penalty. . . . I mean, Fry the bastards. We didn't need a trial; a trial was simply a delay. . . . The police presence around Tim McVeigh and Terry Nichols was the only deterrent that kept me from ending up on death row. Because had I thought there was any opportunity to kill them, I would have done so. . . . But over the next eight months, I remembered a statement that Julie had made to me driving across Iowa one time in her junior year in college. We heard a newscast on the radio about an execution that had happened in Texas the night before. Julie's response was, "Dad, all they're doing is teaching hate to their children in Texas. It has no social redeeming value." . . . After she was killed, this kept echoing in my mind. . . .

One day I went down to the bomb site. . . . I was in deep pain. I was drinking too much, I was smoking three packs of cigarettes a day. . . . The trials hadn't even begun yet, and I went to asking myself, Once they're tried and executed, what then? How's that going to help me? It isn't going to bring Julie back. . . . I realized that it's all about revenge and hate. And revenge and hate was why Julie and 167 others were dead. . . . As I thought about that, I was able to get that revenge and hate out of my system. . . .

The death penalty is about revenge and hate. . . . If we're going to truly follow Christ, as I feel like I try to do, I think we must ask ourselves this one question about the death penalty: Would Jesus pull the switch? I don't think that he would.

On the morality of capital punishment, see the *Catechism of the Catholic Church,* section 2267.

Between Discussions

In Jewish tradition, by the time of Jesus, an approach to the Torah had developed that sought to protect members of the community from violating the divine commands. The approach involved erring on the side of strictness. So, for example, if a particular command was vague, Jewish teachers provided an interpretation that made it more specific. Exodus 20:10 says merely that on the Sabbath, "you shall not do any work." Trying to safeguard people from disobeying this general instruction, some Jewish teachers counseled against such minor labors as casually picking grain heads while strolling through a wheat field (see Mark 2:23–24). A similar strategy guarded against transgressing more specific precepts unwittingly. To ensure that they did not accidentally break the rule that a criminal be given no more than forty lashes, Jews customarily gave only thirty-nine (see 2 Corinthians 11:24). The approach came to be called "putting a fence around the law"—protecting it from violation. Different groups of Jews erected different kinds of fences around the Mosaic law—and sometimes argued with one another about whether the fences were correctly placed.

New Testament scholar Ulrich Luz observes that after Jesus declared his intention to fulfill the Torah right down to its tiniest parts (5:17–20), many of his listeners would have expected him to go on to set up his own fence around the law. Luz points out that Jesus does so, but in a different way from other teachers of his time. The fence that Jesus puts around God's commands is not concerned with quantities. Take, for example, the Old Testament rule of proportionate punishment ("an eye for an eye"). Jesus does not advise us to keep safely away from violating this precept by imposing a punishment on an attacker that is slightly less than the original injury. He does not, for example, instruct us to let the one who strikes twice be struck once in return. Rather, as we have seen, Jesus urges us to strive wholeheartedly for the good, or value, that the precept aims at, which in this case is reconciliation and harmony between people. Thus, Jesus guards us against breaking the "eye for an eye" command by urging us to give up the search for retribution altogether and to do good to the person who harms us. Jesus puts similar fences around the commands not to commit adultery (curb your lustful thoughts) and killing (rein in the anger that leads to violence). Jesus directs us away from a quantitative approach and toward a qualitative approach to God.

Jesus' approach has many implications. For example, if I ask myself, "Where do I stand in regard to the commandment to love God with all my being?" Jesus' sermon seems to suggest that calculating how many minutes I pray each day may not be the best way to answer the question. Perhaps I would learn more about areas in which I need to grow in my relationship with God by examining the preoccupations and anxieties that compete for my energies and attention, draining away my impetus to listen to God's word. I might probe the quality of my relationships with the people around me. By the same token, if I am looking for ways to deepen my relationship with God, adding a few extra minutes to my daily prayer, while it may be a very good thing to do, may not be the most important response I could make to God's command. I might do better to meditate on the beatitudes (5:3–10) and consider what they mean for me.

Similarly, I might ask myself what I should do to better fulfill my duty to support the life and outreach of the church. Putting an extra few dollars in the collection basket each week might be a superficial way to ensure that I am fulfilling my obligation. But Jesus' sermon suggests that I would do better to inquire into the Christian outreaches that are attempting to meet human needs, spiritual and material, in my town and to ask myself what talents and opportunities I have that would enable me to make a contribution to one of them. I could even give my pastor a pleasant surprise by asking him where he thinks I might serve within the activities and ministries of my parish.

Week 4

Just between You and God

Questions to Begin

15 minutes
Use a question or two to get warmed up for the reading.

---

1 When have you enjoyed keeping a secret from someone?

---

2 What is the most difficult thing you ever gave up? Why did you give it up? Did people around you know what you were doing?

Opening the Bible

5 minutes
Read the passage aloud. Let individuals take turns reading paragraphs.

The Reading: Tobit 12:6–10; Matthew 6:1–18

Background: Jewish Tradition on Almsgiving, Prayer, Fasting

Tobit 12:6 "Bless God and acknowledge him in the presence of all the
living for the good things he has done for you. Bless and sing praise to
his name. With fitting honor declare to all people the deeds of God.
Do not be slow to acknowledge him. 7 . . . Do good and evil will not
overtake you. 8 Prayer with fasting is good, but better than both is
almsgiving with righteousness. A little with righteousness is better
than wealth with wrongdoing. It is better to give alms than to lay up
gold. 9 For almsgiving saves from death and purges away every sin.
Those who give alms will enjoy a full life, 10 but those who commit
sin and do wrong are their own worst enemies."

Don't Help Others in Order to Advertise Yourself

Matthew 6:1 "Beware of practicing your piety before others in order to be
seen by them; for then you have no reward from your Father in heaven.

2 "So whenever you give alms, do not sound a trumpet
before you, as the hypocrites do in the synagogues and in the streets,
so that they may be praised by others. Truly I tell you, they have
received their reward. 3 But when you give alms, do not let your left
hand know what your right hand is doing, 4 so that your alms may be
done in secret; and your Father who sees in secret will reward you."

Don't Pray in Order to Enhance Your Reputation

5 "And whenever you pray, do not be like the hypocrites; for they
love to stand and pray in the synagogues and at the street corners, so
that they may be seen by others. Truly I tell you, they have received
their reward. 6 But whenever you pray, go into your room and shut
the door and pray to your Father who is in secret; and your Father
who sees in secret will reward you.

7 "When you are praying, do not heap up empty phrases as
the Gentiles do; for they think that they will be heard because of their
many words. 8 Do not be like them, for your Father knows what you
need before you ask him."

The Lord's Prayer

9 "Pray then in this way:
Our Father in heaven,
hallowed be your name.
10 Your kingdom come.
Your will be done,
on earth as it is in heaven.
11 Give us this day our daily bread.
12 And forgive us our debts,
as we also have forgiven our debtors.
13 And do not bring us to the time of trial,
but rescue us from the evil one.
14 For if you forgive others their trespasses, your heavenly Father will
also forgive you; 15 but if you do not forgive others, neither will your
Father forgive your trespasses."

Don't Fast in Order to Impress Other People

16 "And whenever you fast, do not look dismal, like the hypocrites,
for they disfigure their faces so as to show others that they are fasting.
Truly I tell you, they have received their reward. 17 But when you fast,
put oil on your head and wash your face, 18 so that your fasting may
be seen not by others but by your Father who is in secret; and your
Father who sees in secret will reward you."

Questions for Careful Reading

10 minutes
Choose questions according to your interest and time.

1 Almsgiving, prayer, fasting: what reasons might there be for the order in which Jesus discusses these topics?

2 What is the meaning of the word *hallowed* (6:9)? (Suggested resources: a dictionary and Psalms 96 and 99.)

3 What metaphors for "sins" are used in 6:12, 14–15? How do these metaphors help to explain the nature of sin?

4 What is the reasoning behind the principle Jesus states in 6:14?

5 In what ways is Jesus' model prayer, 6:9–13, different from the approach to prayer that he criticizes in 6:7–8?

6 Fasting is an expression of sorrow. So why should a person who fasts "not look dismal"?

A Guide to the Reading

If participants have not read this section already, read it aloud. Otherwise go on to "Questions for Application."

Jesus has urged us to grasp the purpose of God's commands—to see God's vision of right living and social justice and to put our minds and hearts to the task of pursuing this vision (5:21–48). Similarly, Jesus now urges us to grasp the purpose of religious practices, such as charitable aid, prayer, and fasting. The purpose of these actions is to help us bring ourselves and others closer to God. It is a perversion of religion to engage in these practices to advance our own agendas, to market ourselves to friends, neighbors, business associates, or voters. Religious acts should focus on God. Good deeds should be done in ways that display God's goodness, not ours (5:16; 6:2–3). Prayer should focus on God's purposes for the world, not on our own needs and wants (6:9–10). Penitential practices are a kind of body language for expressing ourselves to God, not a means for gaining other people's admiration (6:16).

6:1. "Beware," Jesus begins. Danger is at hand. Caring for other people's needs, praying, and fasting are normal kinds of behavior for people who seek to live in relationship with God. But whenever we perform these good deeds, questions arise: Who is the audience for my performance? Am I trying to further God's desires or my own? Is my (perhaps unconscious) intention to impress other people? In Greek, "hypocrites" (6:2, 5, 16) are literally actors in a play. Jesus challenges me to ask, "Am I turning religion into theater, with myself in the starring role?"

6:2–4. Our resources are gifts from God. To use them to draw attention to ourselves rather than to God is a slight to the giver. If we neglect to give the credit to the source of our generosity, we can hardly expect our generous deeds to receive any approval from him. Contrast Mother Teresa of Calcutta. When visitors marveled at how much she and her sisters were accomplishing, she would deflect attention from herself and her companions. We're simply doing Jesus' work, she would say.

6:5–15. Notice the sequence of topics: merciful deeds, prayer, fasting. Prayer lies at the center. Without the matrix of personal communion with God through prayer, merciful deeds and self-renunciation become distorted or wither away. In fact, these verses on prayer stand at the center of the entire sermon. Clearly, the message is that we can become righteous and love our neighbor (5:20, 48; 7:12) only by living in communion with God, our Father. Quite simply, Jesus urges us to center our lives on God.

"They love to stand and pray." The people Jesus describes do indeed "love" to pray—but their prayer is a matter of love not for God but for themselves. "Prayer, supposedly the most intimate expression of love to God, has turned into its very opposite, preoccupation with oneself," Hans Dieter Betz remarks.

Go into "your room." For a Galilean listener, this would mean going into the windowless storage room at the back of his or her little farmhouse and standing in the darkness among the hoes and scythes and jars of olive oil. That's *just* the place for talking to God, Jesus affirms.

"Do not heap up empty phrases" and empty "words." In prayer, non-Jews flattered their gods with long lists of titles. Sometimes they used nonsense syllables as a kind of magical speech to get the gods to pay attention to them and come to their aid. The assumption was that gods did not know about humans' needs unless they were specifically informed and might not act on humans' behalf unless they were pressured or manipulated. Jesus rejects such approaches to prayer because he rejects the picture of God that lies behind them. God does not need to be talked into acting on our behalf: he is our Father. And he does not need information about our situation. He already knows us and our needs. Indeed, he knows what we really need better than we do. We are liable to imagine that we need things that are unnecessary or that might do us no good. God, however, knows what would be truly good for us. (For comments on the Our Father, see "Between Discussions," page 64.)

6:16–18. Jews fasted to express mourning, to present their needs to God, and to aid them in purification or meditation. Jesus is not concerned here about *why* we should fast but *for whom.* He advises us to let our fasting be as secret as our prayer in the storage room. Washing and anointing oneself with oil were ordinary practices of hygiene. Thus, Jesus is saying that we should conceal our penitential practices beneath the ordinary exterior of our lives.

Questions for Application

40 minutes
Choose questions according to your interest and time.

---

1 What are some ways in which charitable deeds and charitable giving can be carried out "in secret"?

---

2 Is there a conflict between what Jesus says in 5:14–16 and what he says in 6:3–4? How can the two principles be reconciled in practice?

---

3 Reread 6:5. In what ways is it possible today to make a public display of piety?

---

4 What effects can the refusal to forgive have on the one who refuses to forgive? on the one who is not forgiven?

5 What reward does Jesus urge us to seek from God (6:4, 18)? How does the hope for this reward affect how you live?

6 St. Augustine saw a connection between this reading and the beatitudes. If other people do not praise us for living rightly, Augustine wrote, they are at fault. But if they do praise us, we are in danger—unless we are pure-hearted (5:8). What other connections might there be between the beatitudes and our ability to carry out Jesus' instructions in this week's reading?

Read assiduously and learn as much as you can. Let sleep find you holding your Bible, and when your head nods let it be resting on the sacred page.

St. Jerome, fourth-century biblical scholar

Approach to Prayer

15 minutes
Use this approach—or create your own!

- Pray the Our Father one line at a time, pausing between lines to allow for silent prayer or spontaneous prayers aloud.

  Our Father . . .
  who art in heaven, . . .
  hallowed be thy name; . . .
  thy kingdom come; . . .
  thy will be done on earth as it is in heaven. . . .
  Give us this day our daily bread; . . .
  and forgive us our trespasses . . .
  as we forgive those who trespass against us; . . .
  and lead us not into temptation, . . .
  but deliver us from evil. . . .
  Amen.

  End with a Glory to the Father.

4 *Tobit 12:6–10; Matthew 6:1–18*

Saints in the Making

Generosity without Fanfare

This section is a supplement for individual reading.

The woman who runs an informal ministry out of her back door to the hungry and homeless is a familiar figure in Christian tradition. Not uncommonly, she provokes the ire of family members, who are not pleased at the steady disappearance of their soup and silverware into the hands of unknown (and unneedy?) strangers. Phyllis McGinley captured the type in a poem entitled "The Giveaway," about St. Bridget of Ireland. McGinley wrote: "Saint Bridget drove / The family mad. / For here's the fault in Bridget lay: / She *would* give everything away."

There is a contrasting tradition, however, of women whose menfolk are in on the giveaway. When relatives of Ludwig of Thuringia urged him to get rid of his super-generous wife, Elizabeth, he told them that he wouldn't give her up for a mountain of gold. He supported Elizabeth's wide-ranging charitable projects. Today both are considered saints.

A notable American couple in the Ludwig-and-Elizabeth tradition was the Drexels—Emma Bouvier and her husband, Francis Anthony. Wealthy nineteenth-century Philadelphians—he was a very successful banker—the Drexels were of one mind about aiding needy fellow citizens. Emma provided assistance to many people who, literally, showed up at her back door. She even employed another woman to help her in this service.

Two aspects of Emma Drexel's generosity are especially notable. The first is how quiet she kept it (compare Matthew 6:2–4). Her daughters knew something about her charitable efforts, but even they were astonished to discover after her death that she had been distributing more than twenty thousand dollars a year on a case-by-case basis to needy families. (Multiply that figure by fifteen to bring it up to today's valuation.)

The second remarkable aspect of Emma's—and Francis's—generosity is how it multiplied in the following generation. Their daughters Elizabeth and Louise were noted philanthropists, and Katharine relinquished the personal use of her considerable inheritance and founded a religious congregation, the Sisters of the Blessed Sacrament, devoted to serving Native Americans and African Americans. In 2000, "Mother Drexel" was canonized as the United States' second native-born saint.

Between Discussions

St. Augustine wrote at length on the Our Father in his commentary on the Sermon on the Mount. Here is a selection of his thoughts.

Our Father. When we say "Our Father" to God, love is awakened in us, for what should be more precious to children than their father? Addressing God this way also fosters a humble attitude and a confidence of obtaining what we are about to ask for, since before we ask for anything we have received the great gift of being permitted to say to God, "Our Father." What would he not now give to his asking children, when he has already given them the gift of being his children?

Who art in heaven. That is, you who are in your holy and righteous people. Righteous persons can be called heaven, since it is said to the righteous, "God's temple is holy, and you are that temple" (1 Corinthians 3:17). If God dwells in his temple, and the holy ones are his temple, then "who art in heaven" may rightly be said to equal "who art in your holy ones." The person who says these words wishes that the One to whom he or she prays would indeed dwell also in him or her.

Hallowed be thy name. This is asked not as though God's name were not already holy but so that his name might be regarded as holy by people. And his name is hallowed where it is said with reverence.

Thy kingdom come. This is not said as though God does not reign already, as though he does not reign on earth and has not always reigned on it from the creation of the world! "Thy kingdom come," then, means, "let your reign be manifested to people." For just as a present light is absent to a blind person, so also the reign of God, although it never leaves the earth, is absent to those who are ignorant of it.

Thy will be done on earth as it is in heaven. That is, may your will be in your holy ones who are on earth as it is in the angels who are in heaven, who cling to you in every way and thoroughly enjoy you, without any error clouding their understanding, without any misery interfering with their happiness.

Give us this day our daily bread. We should understand this as spiritual bread, that is, God's commands, which we ought to ponder and put into practice every day. For the Lord said about these commands: "Do not work for the food that perishes, but for the food that endures for eternal life" (John 6:27). However, if anyone wishes to understand this request as referring to the bread that the body needs or to the sacrament of the Lord's body, that person should keep all three meanings together. Thus, in asking for daily bread, he or she asks simultaneously for the bread the body needs and the bread of the visible sacrament and the invisible bread of the word of God.

Forgive us our trespasses as we forgive those who trespass against us. This could be taken to mean that we must forgive only those who ask our forgiveness. But in the instruction by which we are told to pray for our enemies (5:44), we are not told to pray for those who ask our forgiveness—for those who are presently our enemies do not ask for our forgiveness, yet no one can honestly say that he or she prays for those whom he or she does not forgive. For this reason, we must admit that all sins committed against us must be forgiven, if we wish the sins we commit to be forgiven by our Father.

And lead us not into temptation, but deliver us from evil. Here we do not pray that we might not be tempted but that we might not be "brought" into temptation, just as a man who has to be subjected to ordeal by fire would not pray that the fire might not touch him but that it might not burn him. For "the furnace trieth the potter's vessels: and the trial of affliction just men" (Sirach 27:6, Douay-Rheims version). Thus Joseph was tempted by a dishonorable enticement, but he was not "brought" into temptation (Genesis 39:6–12). Susanna was tempted, but neither was she led, or brought, into temptation (Daniel 13:19–27).

Week 5

Look at Your Finances

Questions to Begin

15 minutes
Use a question or two to get warmed up for the reading.

1. When has a sum of money unexpectedly come your way? What was the result?

2. When have you suffered a financial loss? What effect did it have?

Opening the Bible

5 minutes
Read the passage aloud. Let individuals take turns reading paragraphs.

The Reading: Sirach 29:8–13; Matthew 6:19–34; Luke 12:16–21, 33–34

Background: Where Extra Resources Should Go

Sirach 29:8 Be patient with someone in humble circumstances,
and do not keep him waiting for your alms.
9 Help the poor for the commandment's sake,
and in their need do not send them away
empty-handed.
10 Lose your silver for the sake of a brother or a friend,
and do not let it rust under a stone and be lost.
11 Lay up your treasure according to the commandments
of the Most High,
and it will profit you more than gold.
12 Store up almsgiving in your treasury,
and it will rescue you from every disaster;
13 better than a stout shield and a sturdy spear,
it will fight for you against the enemy.

Make a Wise Investment

Matthew 6:19 "Do not store up for yourselves treasures on earth, where
moth and rust consume and where thieves break in and steal; 20 but
store up for yourselves treasures in heaven, where neither moth nor
rust consumes and where thieves do not break in and steal. 21 For
where your treasure is, there your heart will be also."

Envy's Effect on the Envious

22 "The eye is the lamp of the body. So, if your eye is healthy, your
whole body will be full of light; 23 but if your eye is unhealthy, your
whole body will be full of darkness. If then the light in you is
darkness, how great is the darkness!"

A Conflict of Loyalties

24 "No one can serve two masters; for a slave will either hate the one
and love the other, or be devoted to the one and despise the other.
You cannot serve God and wealth."

Let Go and Let God

25 “Therefore I tell you, do not worry about your life, what you will
eat or what you will drink, or about your body, what you will wear. Is
not life more than food, and the body more than clothing? 26 Look at
the birds of the air; they neither sow nor reap nor gather into barns,
and yet your heavenly Father feeds them. Are you not of more value
than they? 27 And can any of you by worrying add a single hour to
your span of life? 28 And why do you worry about clothing? Consider
the lilies of the field, how they grow; they neither toil nor spin, 29 yet
I tell you, even Solomon in all his glory was not clothed like one of
these. 30 But if God so clothes the grass of the field, which is alive
today and tomorrow is thrown into the oven, will he not much more
clothe you—you of little faith? 31 Therefore do not worry, saying,
‘What will we eat?’ or ‘What will we drink?’ or ‘What will we wear?’
32 For it is the Gentiles who strive for all these things; and indeed
your heavenly Father knows that you need all these things. 33 But
strive first for the kingdom of God and his righteousness, and all
these things will be given to you as well.

34 “So do not worry about tomorrow, for tomorrow will
bring worries of its own. Today’s trouble is enough for today.”

A Parable about Surplus Resources

Luke 12:16 Then he told them a parable: “The land of a rich man
produced abundantly. 17 And he thought to himself, ‘What should I
do, for I have no place to store my crops?’ 18 Then he said, ‘I will do
this: I will pull down my barns and build larger ones, and there I will
store all my grain and my goods. 19 And I will say to my soul, “Soul,
you have ample goods laid up for many years; relax, eat, drink, be
merry.”’ 20 But God said to him, ‘You fool! This very night your life is
being demanded of you. And the things you have prepared, whose
will they be?’ 21 So it is with those who store up treasures for
themselves but are not rich toward God.” . . . 33 “Sell your
possessions, and give alms. Make purses for yourselves that do not
wear out, an unfailing treasure in heaven, where no thief comes near
and no moth destroys. 34 For where your treasure is, there your heart
will be also.”

Questions for Careful Reading

10 minutes
Choose questions according to your interest and time.

1 In 6:19, Jesus speaks of moths, corrosion, and burglars as threats to accumulated wealth. What other forces erode wealth?

2 In 6:19–21, is Jesus speaking about gaining wealth or about keeping it, or both? How can you tell?

3 How many different arguments does Jesus offer in 6:25–34 to support his exhortation? Reread the first sentence in 6:25.

4 In 6:26–33, is Jesus telling us not to work and to simply let God provide for us? Judging from 2 Thessalonians 3:6–13, how might St. Paul interpret this section of Jesus' sermon?

5 How would you briefly summarize Jesus' teaching about material resources and material needs?

A Guide to the Reading

If participants have not read this section already, read it aloud. Otherwise go on to "Questions for Application."

From time to time, my daughters interrupt me in conversation to demand, "Is money all you ever think about?" The answer is no, although the fact that they ask the question tells you something. But who can avoid thinking about money? We can never stray far from earning and spending. Often, however, our thinking about money is not mere practical calculation; it reflects fascination and anxiety. Money exercises an influence over us that is out of proportion to its necessity. Money allures us; it competes with God for first place in our lives. This struggle for priority is the focus in this week's portion of the sermon.

6:19–21. "Do not store up for yourselves treasures on earth." More literally, Jesus says, "Don't be storing up . . ." He assumes that everyone seeks to maximize his or her material advantages.

As he did earlier in the sermon, Jesus states his views in an abbreviated manner. Here he speaks of divesting ourselves of surplus wealth but does not state what should be done with it. He assumes that his listeners are acquainted with Jewish tradition, which held that well-heeled people should not hold on to their wealth, because poor people cannot survive unless resources are shared out (see the reading from Sirach). Jesus makes the connection between not hoarding and aiding those in need at the conclusion of his parable in Luke: "Sell your possessions, and give alms" (Luke 12:33).

6:22–23. Jesus' words about light and eyes are puzzling, and scholarly explanations tend to be complicated. Since the context concerns money, we may suppose that these words also have something to do with our relationship with material things. "If your eye is unhealthy" is more literally "if your eye is evil." The concept of the "evil eye" was common in the ancient Near East. Giving someone the "evil eye" meant looking at them with envy (a look that, many thought, actually caused harm). Thus Jesus may be contrasting an attitude of generosity toward others (a "healthy" or "sincere" eye) with an attitude of envy and greed. He implies that we should perform eye exams on ourselves.

6:24. For *wealth* the Greek text uses an Aramaic word, *mammon.* This term referred to wealth as a kind of pseudogod, a personified, almost demonic force. The term brings out the struggle for our loyalty that rages in us between God and material riches. Clearly Jesus expects us to demonstrate our loyalty to God in how we use our money.

Jesus has been training us to discover God's purposes and pursue them with determination (5:21–6:18). What is God's purpose for our material resources? A clue lies in the fact that Jesus puts his instruction about money between his call to imitate God's generosity (5:44–45, 48) and his call to care for our neighbors as we would like them to care for us (7:12). God's purpose for our material resources is to meet human needs. Jesus does not lay down rules for how exactly we should fulfill this purpose. He simply points to the principle and leaves us to decide how to implement it. It might have been easier if Jesus had given us a guideline specifying the percentage of our income we should spend on ourselves and the percentage we should distribute to others, but he did not. Each of us has to listen to his words and then go into our own back room (6:6) and, in the presence of our Father, who knows what we need, ponder what we should do in response.

6:25–34. Materialism shows itself not only in jealousy and envy (6:22–23) and in holding on to resources we don't need (6:19–21) but also in worrying about whether we will have enough. Jesus reminds us that God made us to live for things more important than food and clothing (verse 25). This raises the question of what we *are* supposed to live for. The answer is given in verse 33.

St. Augustine notes that Jesus does not tell us to seek God's kingdom *and* material things equally. That would be trying to serve two masters. Rather, Augustine says, we are to seek material things *to the extent that* they enable us to serve the coming of God's kingdom. Jesus tells us to focus on furthering God's project of righteousness and justice in the world (verse 33) and to leave to God not only the fulfillment of our needs but even the determination of what our needs really are.

Questions for Application

40 minutes
Choose questions according to your interest and time.

1. Where is the dividing line between storing up treasure on earth and obtaining the material resources you need for your life?

2. Have you ever envied someone and then discovered that it made no sense to envy them? If so, what did you learn from the experience? Most of us enjoy hearing about the messed-up lives of the rich and famous. Why do we enjoy it?

3. What is envy's impact on the one who envies?

4. Reread 6:24. How is it possible to grow in serving God rather than wealth? Where do you feel this conflict between serving God and serving wealth? What is holding you back from serving God?

5 What steps can a person who is worried about money take to respond to Jesus' encouragement not to worry (6:25–34)?

6 How can Christians help one another respond to Jesus' teaching in this week's reading? Can you help someone who's worried about money? Can you help the poor in a concrete way?

7 For private reflection on 6:22–23: Are your perceptions of others darkened by a desire to have what they have? Do you feel a twinge of unhappiness at the good things that other people enjoy? What decision is Jesus inviting you to make about your attitude toward material things?

Bible reading must be our ordinary, everyday food, because it is the only way we can learn who God is, who we are, and what the meaning of our life in this world is.

Cardinal Joseph Ratzinger, German theologian and head of the Vatican's Congregation for the Doctrine of the Faith

Approach to Prayer

15 minutes
Use this approach—or create your own!

- Pray together—or take turns praying verse by verse—Psalm 63:1–8 and Psalm 65. End with a Glory to the Father.

5 | *Sirach 29:8–13; Matthew 6:19–34; Luke 12:16–21, 33–34*

Saints in the Making

The Monastic Movement Begins

This section is a supplement for individual reading.

St. Anthony, who lived from around 251 to 356, spearheaded the monastic movement, which sprang up in Egypt and quickly spread to the rest of the Church. His decision to go into the desert to devote himself to prayer was precipitated by a passage in our reading this week. Here is the narrative of Anthony's first biographer, St. Athanasius.

After the death of his father and mother, Anthony was left alone with one little sister: [Anthony's] age was about twenty, and on him the care of his sister rested. Six months after the death of his parents, going according to custom into the Lord's house . . . it happened the Gospel was being read, and he heard the Lord saying to the rich man, "If you wish to be perfect, go, sell your possessions, and give the money to the poor, and you will have treasure in heaven; then come, follow me" (19:21). As though the passage had been read on his account, Anthony went out immediately from the church and gave his inherited lands—some three hundred productive acres—to the villagers. The rest that was movable he sold and gave the proceeds to the poor, reserving a little, however, for his sister. Again as he went into church, hearing the Lord say in the Gospel, "Do not worry about tomorrow" (6:34), he went out and gave those things also to the poor. Entrusting his sister to faithful virgins to be brought up, he devoted himself to discipline, training himself with patience. . . .

Anthony at first began to abide in places outside the village. Then, if he heard of a good man anywhere, like the prudent bee, he went forth and sought him and returned, having got from the good man, as it were, supplies for his journey on the way of virtue. He decided not to return to the village of his kinsfolk, but to keep all his desire and energy for perfecting his discipline. He worked, however, with his hands, having heard, "Anyone unwilling to work should not eat" (2 Thessalonians 3:10), and part he spent on bread and part he gave to the needy. He was constant in prayer, knowing that a person ought to pray in secret unceasingly (6:6; 1 Thessalonians 5:17). For he gave such heed to what was read that he remembered all, and afterwards his memory served him for books.

Between Discussions

Jesus began his sermon with "beatitudes"—congratulations to the men and women who take his road through life and assurance that the road leads to happiness. Having now read through most of the sermon, we can understand why Jesus prefaced it with this reassurance. The road that Jesus is recommending is full of risks!

The risks are glaringly apparent in Jesus' teaching on how to conduct our relationships with other people. In his antitheses (5:21–48), he urges us to put our welfare and security on the line in the pursuit of harmony, justice, and peace. His approaches to dealing with spouses, friends, strangers, and enemies are designed to maximize the possibilities for maintaining good relationships and healing broken ones. Yet Jesus does not provide any guarantees that these approaches will actually succeed. The outcome always depends on the response of the other party, who is free to respond as he or she wants. If we refuse to indulge in anger, if we offer forgiveness, if we show kindness to an opponent, we may succeed in overcoming evil, in burying the hatchet. But our generosity may sometimes be met with cynical exploitation.

If our efforts do not meet with willingness on the part of others to achieve justice and peace, we stand to lose. If it becomes known that I am reluctant to go to court (following 5:25), will the people with whom I do business cheat me, knowing that I am unlikely to sue them for damages? Suppose I am embroiled in a bitter conflict with my wife. If she knows that I am strongly disinclined to seek a divorce (and that, if we divorce, I would not regard myself as free to remarry—5:31–32), will she take advantage of me? What if someone at work does something to undermine my career, and I don't retaliate (5:38–42)? Won't that person go on to do something worse to me?

Jesus' teaching about material resources and material needs also involves taking risks. He advises us to abandon the search for material security and to focus instead on serving God's kingdom, trusting that God will care for our material needs (6:19–21, 31–33). While Jesus stresses that God will provide for us (6:25–32), this assurance stands alongside his acknowledgment that people who are doing God's will sometimes suffer poverty and deprivation (5:3, 10). Thus Jesus' call to trust God with the material aspect of our lives does not carry a literal guarantee that we will never suffer want.

The Sermon on the Mount is an invitation to dangerous living. Jesus sketches a way of life that is appealing in its simplicity, in its earnest desire for social harmony, in its freedom from anxiety. Yet it is frightening in its vulnerability to pain and loss. Jesus' instructions must give pause to any sensible person. Indeed, Jesus himself encourages us to prudently consider the difficulties we may encounter on the journey he proposes (7:14; Luke 9:57–58; 14:25–33).

It is helpful to recall that the risky elements of Jesus' preaching are part of his announcement of good news—"good news" being the meaning of *gospel.* Jesus presents his risky way of life as a response to a new phase of God's activity in the world. The keynote of Jesus' ministry is his announcement that "the kingdom of heaven has come near" (4:17). Jesus proclaims that with his own coming, God has begun to act in a deeper, more powerful way among human beings—and that this new phase of God's activity will ultimately culminate in the complete arrival of a condition of justice and peace in God's presence. Jesus' sermon tells us how to live in a way that is attuned to the present stirrings of God's kingdom. He teaches us how to catch the wave of God's present activity and ride it in to the eternal shore.

Thus the risks that Jesus invites us to take are a response to God's initiative. Jesus calls us to set aside our preoccupation with our own needs and to direct our energies toward the coming of God's kingdom (6:33), since that is exactly what God himself is doing.

Postscript: I showed the above reflections to a friend of mine, George Mendenhall, a scholar who has spent his life studying the ancient Near East. In response to my observation that living the Sermon on the Mount is risky business, he made this comment: "It might be worthwhile to point out that there are even greater risks in following the way of the world: world wars, mass destruction, wholesale mass murder, and, repeatedly in the ancient world, temporary (only two or three centuries) ends to civilization."

Week 6

Which House Are You Building?

Questions to Begin

15 minutes
Use a question or two to get warmed up for the reading.

---

1 What was the nicest home you ever lived in? What did you like about it?

---

2 When have you been taken in by a sales pitch and regretted it afterward?

Opening the Bible

5 minutes
Read the passage aloud. Let individuals take turns reading paragraphs.

The Reading: Matthew 7

Self-Criticism Comes First

7:1 "Do not judge, so that you may not be judged. 2 For with the
judgment you make you will be judged, and the measure you give will
be the measure you get. 3 Why do you see the speck in your
neighbor's eye, but do not notice the log in your own eye? 4 Or how
can you say to your neighbor, 'Let me take the speck out of your eye,'
while the log is in your own eye? 5 You hypocrite, first take the log
out of your own eye, and then you will see clearly to take the speck
out of your neighbor's eye."

Puzzling Advice

6 "Do not give what is holy to dogs; and do not throw your pearls
before swine, or they will trample them under foot and turn and
maul you."

More Instruction on Prayer

7 "Ask, and it will be given you; search, and you will find; knock, and
the door will be opened for you. 8 For everyone who asks receives,
and everyone who searches finds, and for everyone who knocks, the
door will be opened. 9 Is there anyone among you who, if your child
asks for bread, will give a stone? 10 Or if the child asks for a fish, will
give a snake? 11 If you then, who are evil, know how to give good
gifts to your children, how much more will your Father in heaven give
good things to those who ask him!"

The Golden Rule

12 "In everything do to others as you would have them do to you; for
this is the law and the prophets."

Final Warnings

13 "Enter through the narrow gate; for the gate is wide and the road
is easy that leads to destruction, and there are many who take it.
14 For the gate is narrow and the road is hard that leads to life, and
there are few who find it.

15 "Beware of false prophets, who come to you in sheep's
clothing but inwardly are ravenous wolves. 16 You will know them by
their fruits. Are grapes gathered from thorns, or figs from thistles?
17 In the same way, every good tree bears good fruit, but the bad tree
bears bad fruit. 18 A good tree cannot bear bad fruit, nor can a bad
tree bear good fruit. 19 Every tree that does not bear good fruit is cut
down and thrown into the fire. 20 Thus you will know them by their
fruits.

21 "Not everyone who says to me, 'Lord, Lord,' will enter
the kingdom of heaven, but only the one who does the will of my
Father in heaven. 22 On that day many will say to me, 'Lord, Lord,
did we not prophesy in your name, and cast out demons in your
name, and do many deeds of power in your name?' 23 Then I will
declare to them, 'I never knew you; go away from me, you evildoers.'

24 "Everyone then who hears these words of mine and acts
on them will be like a wise man who built his house on rock. 25 The
rain fell, the floods came, and the winds blew and beat on that house,
but it did not fall, because it had been founded on rock. 26 And
everyone who hears these words of mine and does not act on them
will be like a foolish man who built his house on sand. 27 The rain
fell, and the floods came, and the winds blew and beat against that
house, and it fell—and great was its fall!"

28 Now when Jesus had finished saying these things, the
crowds were astounded at his teaching, 29 for he taught them as one
having authority, and not as their scribes.

Questions for Careful Reading

10 minutes
Choose questions according to your interest and time.

1 What other words might be substituted for *judge* in 7:1–2 in order to bring out Jesus' meaning?

2 What does 7:6 suggest about the way people in Jesus' culture thought about dogs? What animal might Jesus have used if he were to make his statement today?

3 Considering what Jesus has said earlier in the sermon, what might be the "good things" for which he encourages us to ask God (7:7–11)?

4 Again considering what Jesus has said earlier in the sermon, what are the good and bad fruits in 7:16–20? How can 7:15–20 be interpreted and applied, given the phenomenon that Jesus refers to in 6:2, 5, 16?

5 What do the rains and floods in 7:24–27 symbolize?

A Guide to the Reading

If participants have not read this section already, read it aloud. Otherwise go on to "Questions for Application."

7:1–2. "Do not judge." Jesus does not forbid juries to deliver verdicts or critics to write book reviews. He targets our tendency to belittle others, to criticize harshly or unfairly, without sympathy and understanding. St. Augustine interpreted Jesus' words to mean that we should not make "rash judgments"; that is, we should not make negative evaluations of people's motives when their motives are not obvious or write people off as beyond hope of improvement. Again, Jesus is concerned with peace and harmony between people.

"Do not judge, so that you may not be judged" (7:1). Judgmental statements about other people set up a vicious cycle. "Gossipers become targets of gossip; critics must face being criticized, and so forth," Hans Dieter Betz points out. "The prudent person . . . will break the vicious cycle by withholding such judgment. . . . Restraint will motivate others to exercise equal restraint."

7:3–5. Jesus does not intend to eliminate constructive criticism but to eliminate the reason why so much criticism fails to be constructive: our lack of awareness of our own faults and weaknesses. If we cannot see our own flaws, we are incapable of helping anyone else see theirs. Ulrich Luz remarks, "Whoever has a log in the eye is completely blind and therefore cannot at all judge concerning the splinter in the eye of the neighbor!" Augustine remarks that before we offer someone criticism, we should ask ourselves whether we have made the same kind of mistake he or she is making. If we have not, we should acknowledge that it is the kind of mistake that we *could* make, given our human weakness. If we have made the mistake ourselves, we should show compassion rather than harshness. And if we still fall into the same fault, we should invite our brother or sister to join us in a common effort to change.

7:6. Jesus' words about pearls and swine are mysterious (compare Proverbs 11:22). The earliest interpretation is found in the *Didache,* a Christian writing from the end of the first century: "Let no one eat or drink from your eucharistic meal except those who were baptized in the name of the Lord, for about this matter the Lord said, 'Do not give the holy to the dogs.'"

7:7–11. Ask, seek, knock: Jesus' words on prayer are linked to his earlier teaching on the subject (6:7–13). There he instructed us to focus our prayers on the coming of God's just and peaceful kingdom rather than on our own needs, about which God is already well-informed; here he assures us that God will answer our prayers. Our Father will give "good things" to those who ask him. Jesus does not lead us to assume that God will give us simply whatever we request but that he will give us what is good for us. In a later scene, Jesus himself makes a heartfelt request to God (26:36–46): he prays for life, and God grants his request—not by preserving him from death but by raising him from the dead.

It is jarring to hear Jesus address his listeners as "you . . . who are evil." But in most cases in Scripture, this is not a sweeping condemnation of human beings but a way of emphasizing the contrast between humans and the good God (see 19:17).

7:12. Jesus concludes the body of his sermon with the Golden Rule. The Golden Rule expresses the heart of the Old Testament teaching. At the same time, the Old Testament teaching clarifies the meaning of the Golden Rule: we should not do to others simply whatever might accord with our own opinions and preferences; rather, we should treat others with the integrity and compassion that God reveals in Scripture. Jesus instructs us not simply to refrain from injuring others (do not do to others what you wish others would not do to you); rather, he urges us to do good. We should imitate God, who takes the initiative to give us life and bless us with good things.

7:13–27. Jesus closes his sermon with a warning: Everything depends on our choosing to follow his instructions (7:13–14, 24–27). Failure is possible. Indeed, "few" will reach the goal. And those who do reach the goal will be the ones who actually travel the road that Jesus has marked out, not those who have merely memorized the road map. Good theology alone (knowing that Jesus is "Lord"—7:21–22) is not enough.

With so much riding on our choice, it is crucial for us to avoid deception by others (7:15–20) and self-deception (7:21–23). Indeed, Jesus' entire sermon steers us away from delusions about the purpose of life (and delusions about our own holiness) and shows us the path toward lasting happiness.

Questions for Application

40 minutes
Choose questions according to your interest and time.

1 When have you received constructive criticism? What made it helpful? How did it help you? What did it teach you about offering criticism and suggestions to others?

2 When have you realized that you felt critical toward someone else for something that is a weakness or fault in yourself? How did this realization affect you?

3 Jesus urges persistence in prayer (7:7–11). On a scale of one to ten, how would you rate yourself in this regard? What invitation from the Lord does this passage contain for you?

4 What is one simple, specific, concrete way in which you could put the Golden Rule (7:12) into practice in the coming week?

5 In 7:15–20, Jesus warns against being deceived by others. In 7:21–23 he warns against self-deception. In what ways might self-delusion set us up for being deluded by others? Have you experienced this dynamic?

6 How might Jesus' instructions in the sermon apply to driving—for example, turning the other cheek? not judging? Are you a Sermon-on-the-Mount driver?

7 What has been the most important message for you in the Sermon on the Mount? How will you continue to respond to that message?

Bread is converted into nourishment only by breaking and chewing it, just as Scripture feeds the soul by being opened up and discussed.

St. Augustine, *The Lord's Sermon on the Mount*

Approach to Prayer

15 minutes
Use this approach—or create your own!

- Pray a Hail Mary. Then allow time for silent reflection and spontaneous prayers in response to anything in the Sermon on the Mount. To conclude, pray together either Psalm 1 or the Our Father.

Saints in the Making

Stop Judging!

This section is a supplement for individual reading.

The following was written by Sister Ann Shields, the superior of the Servants of God's Love, a Catholic charismatic religious community in the diocese of Lansing, Michigan.

Some years ago I said a dangerous prayer: "God, I don't want to be judging people rashly, as I do. Whatever you have to do to change me, do it."

The next day I was on a plane, sitting in an aisle seat. A man sitting somewhat in front of me was speaking. He had a cup of coffee in his hand and was waving it around.

"Look at him," I thought. "He's going to hit somebody with that cup. Somebody's going to get scalded. You'd think he'd be more careful."

Sure enough, a flight attendant walked down the aisle, and the man bumped her. Hot coffee spilled all down her dress. I sat back smugly. "Of course."

About twenty minutes later I felt like having a cup of coffee—which was unusual for me—and I asked for one. A man across the aisle asked me a question. I am one of those people who cannot talk without using my hands. I began gesturing with the cup in my hand. Another flight attendant came down the aisle, I bumped her, and hot coffee spilled all over her too. I heard the Lord say, "Ahem."

Ever since I have prayed that prayer, it seems that whenever I have rashly jumped to a negative judgment of someone, before the day is out I have done the very same thing for which I judged them.

A Remaining Question or Two

"When Jesus had finished saying these things," Matthew tells us at the end of the Sermon on the Mount, "the crowds were astounded at his teaching" (7:28). We can well imagine that the crowd was astounded, and his disciples even more so. By becoming his followers, they had implicitly agreed to put his instructions into practice. Now he was directing them to adopt a radically God-centered life—so radical that it seemed to go against the grain of human nature. Forget about accumulating material wealth. Curb all sexual desires outside marriage. Show kindness to your enemies. Quite likely the disciples voiced the kind of protest they expressed later, when Jesus further clarified his position on wealth: "They were greatly astounded and said, 'Then who can be saved?'" (19:25).

Jesus' followers in every later generation have shared his first disciples' amazement. Only if we read Jesus' sermon in "a pious coma"—to use the phrase of twentieth-century Catholic writer Frank Sheed—can we come away without sharing their amazement. Over the centuries, Christians pondering the challenge of Jesus' sermon have produced enough books to fill a library. In these remaining pages, I offer a few thoughts on a couple of issues raised by Jesus' words. Perhaps my remarks will spur you to think further about the sermon on your own.

A big question about the Sermon on the Mount is whether it applies to the spheres of government, law, and relations between states. Does Jesus' teaching against retaliation (5:38–42) rule out criminal-justice systems? Does loving our enemies (5:44) mean that under no circumstances may nations go to war?

Jesus does not address these issues directly in his sermon. He does indicate that God did not give the commands of the Torah primarily to show how legal systems should operate or how political authority should be exercised. The Torah chiefly instructs us in how to be the kind of people God has created us to be—people who, like God, do good to human beings out of an unlimited desire for their welfare (5:44–48). We miss the basic purpose of the Torah if we view it as a catalog of crimes to be avoided or a collection of principles for a judicial system that limits wrongdoing through the use of government power. In the Sermon on the Mount, Jesus calls to us to commit ourselves to seeking God's justice in the way we live.

At the same time, Jesus does not deny that legal systems are necessary for moving society at least a little toward justice. For example, Jesus insists that the Torah command "you shall not murder" *primarily* directs us to seek justice and peace in our relationships with other people, but he does not deny that civil society should have laws against murder.

In fact, Jesus does not set any limit on the realms in which we should apply his teaching. He never suggests that it is applicable only to private matters and relationships. Nothing in the world is excluded from God's concern (5:45; 6:26–30). Hence, no sphere of life is excluded from our responsibility to seek righteousness (5:6, 13–16). It is reasonable to conclude that Jesus intends us to apply his teaching about righteousness and love of neighbor to the social and political realms.

Yet Jesus does not give us specific directions for how to apply his teaching to the large spheres of government and economics. But then, neither does he tell us exactly how to apply his teaching to the smaller spheres in which we live. Jesus gives us freedom and responsibility. We are free to determine how to apply his teaching to the various spheres of our existence—and we have the responsibility to use this freedom well.

It is worth noting that the responsibility to apply Jesus' teaching to the realms of government, law, and so on weighs on us more heavily than it did on his first disciples. The limited technology of the ancient world severely restricted the ways in which social and economic problems could be ameliorated. Limitations on ordinary people's access to political power prevented most people from having any influence on government structures and policies. In contrast, many of us today do have the opportunity to play at least a modest role in helping to deal with social and economic problems, through both political and private means. Blessed are we if we hunger and thirst for righteousness not just in our own hearts and homes but in our nation and world.

Obviously, numerous questions arise regarding how to apply Jesus' teaching in the Sermon on the Mount to the realms of politics and economics. A bridge connecting Jesus' simple, radical instructions in Matthew 5–7 to the complexities of the twenty-first century can be constructed only with careful theological, philosophical, and practical thinking. Building such a bridge is more than any of us could accomplish in a lifetime—yet the responsibility to live out Jesus' teaching presses on us here and now. Here the Church's tradition of reflection and action is an invaluable resource.

If you are unfamiliar with Catholic social teaching, you have an enriching surprise in store. To explore this resource, I would suggest you begin by reading the dozen or so pages on "human community" in the *Catechism of the Catholic Church* (sections 1877–1948; and see 2244). Then, for examples of how the basic principles might be applied to particular situations, you might take a look at the United States Bishops' Web site (http://www.usccb.org/socialjustice.htm). John Paul II has applied the tradition of Catholic social thought to contemporary situations in several encyclicals, which can be viewed at the Vatican Web site (http://www.vatican.va/holy_father/john_paul_ii/encyclicals/). The style of Church documents is often stiff and formal, but the content is often accessible. Overall, the Church's social teaching is an invaluable resource for anyone seeking to discover Christian approaches to the tangled issues of justice and peace in our world.

Of course, while the tradition points the way toward dealing with modern issues in a truly Christian way, it does not try to answer all the specific questions that arise about how to apply Jesus' teaching to a constantly changing world. Each of us is left with much hard thinking to do.

A second question about the Sermon on the Mount has shadowed us throughout our reading: Where is grace?

Jesus summons us to action. He makes it quite clear that intentions and words without a change of heart and corresponding deeds constitute a path to eternal destruction (7:13–14, 21–27). Those who merely write books or engage in discussions about the beatitudes are not in a good position with regard to the coming kingdom of God. Jesus congratulates those who actually *live* his lifestyle of poverty of spirit, purity of heart, and so on (5:3–10). Jesus even seems to raise the bar: unless our response to God surpasses mediocre, self-serving piety, we will not gain admission to God's kingdom (5:20, 43–48).

The demands that Jesus makes of us may leave us gasping for breath. Who can truly live the life of the Sermon on the Mount? Surely it can be only men and women who have access to a source of strength that is greater than their puny human resources. Jesus calls us to imitate God, to do God's deeds, to live God's life on earth (5:16, 44–45, 48). We can do so only if God shares his own righteousness and love with us. But where in the Sermon on the Mount can we find the divine grace to live this life?

If we were to ask St. Luke or St. Paul, they would probably answer, "Through the presence of the Holy Spirit in us!" Matthew, I am sure, would not disagree; but he seems to have put his answer in a different form. Matthew's answer, as I see it, is that it is in the Speaker that we find the grace to live a Sermon-on-the-Mount life. Matthew shows us that Jesus' birth, baptism, and temptation demonstrate that he is the unique, obedient Son of God. Thus he himself is the source of help for those who wish to live as God's obedient sons and daughters. Jesus makes this point later in the Gospel, when he declares that it is by being "yoked" to him—like two oxen yoked together to draw a plow—that we will find rest and refreshment in the midst of the toil and weariness of living out his way of life (11:28–30). In addition, Jesus' teaching to his disciples about how to live as his community (for example, chapter 18) suggests that it is in his community that we will find support, example, and encouragement to continue on his path. This is so because Jesus continues to be in his community: the risen Jesus is "Emmanuel," that is, "God-with-us" (1:23). In his final words in the Gospel, Jesus charges his followers to teach his way of life—meaning, above all, his teaching in the Sermon on the Mount—and assures us that he will be with us to the end of the age (28:19–20). Jesus himself—God-with-us—is the gift of God's grace. He enables us to live the life that leads to happiness.

Like a camping trip, a Bible discussion group works best if you agree on where you're going and how you intend to get there. Many groups use their first meeting to talk over such questions and reach a consensus. Here is a checklist of issues, with bits of advice from people who have experience in Bible discussions. (A planning discussion will go more smoothly if the leaders have thought through the following issues beforehand.)

Agree on your purpose. Are you getting together to gain wisdom and direction for your lives? to finally get acquainted with the Bible? to support one another in following Christ? to encourage those who are exploring—or reexploring—the Church? for other reasons?

Agree on attitudes. For example: "We're all beginners here." "We're here to help each other understand and respond to God's word." "We're not here to offer counseling or direction to one another." "We want to read Scripture prayerfully." What do *you* wish to emphasize? Make it explicit!

Agree on ground rules. Barbara J. Fleischer, in her useful book *Facilitating for Growth*, recommends that a group clearly state its approach to the following:

- *Preparation.* Do we agree to read the material and prepare the answers to the questions before each meeting?
- *Attendance.* What kind of priority will we give to our meetings?
- *Self-revelation.* Are we willing to help the others in the group gradually get to know us—our weaknesses as well as our strengths, our needs as well as our gifts?
- *Listening.* Will we commit ourselves to listening to one another?
- *Confidentiality.* Will we keep everything that is shared *with* the group *in* the group?
- *Discretion.* Will we refrain from sharing about the faults and sins of people who are not in the group?
- *Encouragement and support.* Will we give as well as receive?
- *Participation.* Will we give each person time and opportunity to make a contribution?

You could probably take a pen and draw a circle around listening and *confidentiality.* Those two points are especially important.

The following items could be added to Fleischer's list:

- *Relationship with parish.* Is our group part of the adult faith-formation program? independent but operating with the express approval of the pastor? not a parish-based group?
- *New members.* Will we let new members join us once we have begun the six weeks of discussions?

Agree on housekeeping.

- *When will we meet?*
- *How often will we meet?* Meeting weekly or every other week is best if you can manage it. William Riley remarks, "Meetings once a month are too distant from each other for the threads of the last session not to be lost" *(The Bible Study Group: An Owner's Manual).*
- *How long will meetings run?*
- *Where will we meet?*
- *Is any setup needed?* Christine Dodd writes that "the problem with meeting in a place like a church hall is that it can be very soul-destroying" given the cold, impersonal feel of many church facilities. If you have to meet in a church facility, Dodd recommends doing something to make the area homey *(Making Scripture Work).*
- *Who will host the meetings?* Leaders and hosts are not necessarily the same people.
- *Will we have refreshments?* Who will provide them?
- *What about child care?* Most experienced leaders of Bible discussion groups discourage bringing infants or other children to adult Bible discussions.

Agree on leadership. You need someone to facilitate—to keep the discussion on track, to see that everyone has a chance to speak, to help the group stay on schedule. Rena Duff, editor of the newsletter *Sharing God's Word Today,* recommends having two or three people take turns leading the discussions.

It's okay if the leader is not an expert on the Bible. You have this booklet, and if questions come up that no one can answer, you can delegate a participant to do a little research between meetings. It's important for the leader to set an example of listening, to draw out the quieter members (and occasionally restrain the more vocal ones), to move the group on when it gets stuck, to remind the members of their agreements, and to summarize what the group is accomplishing.

Bible discussion is an opportunity to experience the fulfillment of Jesus' promise "Where two or three are gathered in my name, I am there among them" (Matthew 18:20). Put your discussion group in Jesus' hands. Pray for the guidance of the Spirit. And have a great time exploring God's word together!

Suggestions for Individuals

You can use this booklet just as well for individual study as for group discussion. While discussing the Bible with other people can be a rich experience, there are advantages to reading on your own. For example:

- You can focus on the points that interest you most.
- You can go at your own pace.
- You can be completely relaxed and unashamedly honest in your answers to all the questions, since you don't have to share them with anyone!

My suggestions for using this booklet on your own are these:

- Don't skip "Questions to Begin." The questions can help you as an individual reader to warm up to the topic of the reading.
- Take your time on "Questions for Careful Reading" and "Questions for Application." While a group will probably not have enough time to work on all the questions, you can allow yourself the time to consider all of them if you are using the booklet by yourself.
- After reading the "Guide to the Reading," go back and reread the Scripture text before doing the "Questions for Application."
- Take the time to look up all the parenthetical Scripture references.
- Since you control the pace, give yourself plenty of opportunities to reflect on the meaning of the Sermon on the Mount for you. Let your reading be an opportunity for these words to become God's words to you.

Resources

Bibles

The following editions of the Bible contain the full set of biblical books recognized by the Catholic Church, along with a great deal of useful explanatory material:

- The Catholic Study Bible (Oxford University Press), which uses the text of the New American Bible
- The Catholic Bible: Personal Study Edition (Oxford University Press), which also uses the text of the New American Bible
- The New Jerusalem Bible, the regular (not the reader's) edition (Doubleday)

Books, Web Sites, and Other Resources

- St. Augustine, *The Lord's Sermon on the Mount,* Ancient Christian Writers, no. 5, trans. John J. Jepson, S.S. (Westminster, Md.: Newman Press, 1948). (Note: certain of Augustine's views on Jews, women, and the body need careful interpretation.)
- Daniel J. Harrington, S.J., *The Gospel of Matthew,* Sacra Pagina (Collegeville, Minn.: Liturgical Press, 1991).
- John P. Meier, *Matthew,* New Testament Message (Wilmington, Del.: Michael Glazier, 1980).
- George T. Montague, S.M., *Companion God: A Cross-Cultural Commentary on the Gospel of Matthew* (New York: Paulist Press, 1989).
- For more information on Pier Giorgio Frassati, visit http://www.piergiorgiofrassati.org
- For more information on St. Katharine Drexel, visit http://www.katharinedrexel.org

How has Scripture had an impact on your life? Was this booklet helpful to you in your study of the Bible? Please send comments, suggestions, and personal experiences to Kevin Perrotta, c/o Trade Editorial Department, Loyola Press, 3441 N. Ashland Ave., Chicago, IL 60657.